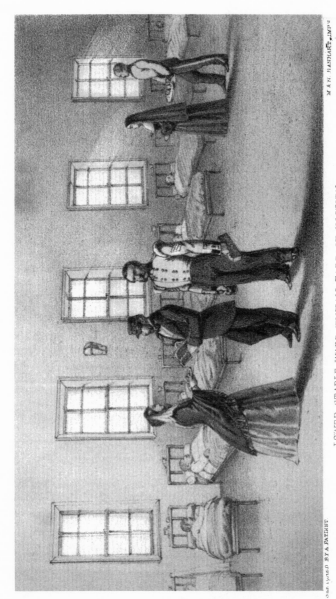

Copyrighted BY A PATENT

MAN RANHARTp IMP?

LOWER STABLE WARD, KOULALI BARRACK HOSPITAL.

London Hurst & Blackett. 1856

EASTERN HOSPITALS

AND

ENGLISH NURSES;

THE NARRATIVE OF

TWELVE MONTHS' EXPERIENCE

IN THE

HOSPITALS OF KOULALI AND SCUTARI.

BY

A LADY VOLUNTEER.

"They are the patient sorrows that touch nearest."—ION.

IN TWO VOLUMES.
VOL. II.

The Naval & Military Press Ltd

in association with

The National Army Museum, London

Published jointly by

The Naval & Military Press Ltd
Unit 10 Ridgewood Industrial Park,
Uckfield, East Sussex,
TN22 5QE England

Tel: +44 (0) 1825 749494
Fax: +44 (0) 1825 765701

www.naval-military-press.com
www.military-genealogy.com
www.militarymaproom.com

and

The National Army Museum, London
www.national-army-museum.ac.uk

Printed and bound in Great Britain by
CPI Antony Rowe, Chippenham and Eastbourne
*In reprinting in facsimile from the original, any imperfections are inevitably reproduced
and the quality may fall short of modern type and cartographic standards.*

CONTENTS.

CHAPTER I.

CHAPTER II.

CONTENTS.

CHAPTER VI.

EASTERN HOSPITALS

AND

ENGLISH NURSES.

CHAPTER I.

Improvements in the hospital—The medical and purveying departments—Difficulties and impossibilities
—Our wants and the manner in which they were
supplied—Mr. Robertson—The results of his exertions—Charcoal brasiers—Etnas—Construction of
the ladies' ward-rooms—Ripe fruit for the sick—A
box from England—Pictures of the past—The "Fresh
Arrivals"—Soldiers' letters and their directions—The
conduct of the hired nurses—The ladies lay aside
the government costume—Necessity of some distinction between the hired nurses and the ladies—
Fresh arrivals and fresh troubles—A manœuvre for a
free passage—Sad scandals—Misbehaviour of the
hired nurses—Mrs. Woodward an exception.

Up to this period the improvements in the
hospital had been slow and unsatisfactory,

and were owing more to the merciful cessation of death and suffering than to any exertions on the part of the authorities; to this we must except the medical staff, who, as far as our knowledge went, exerted themselves to provide all the remedies and create all the improvements they could consistently with the routine of their work; but this routine was so rigid that many necessary improvements fell short of its scope.

The two departments of the army who have most concern with its hospitals are the medical and the purveying ones, the commissariat belonging only to the army in the field. Up to May, 1854, the purveying department continued in a most inefficient state. Requisitions on the stores for necessary articles were constantly dishonoured, while anything out of the common routine was never to be thought of.

Of course in Turkey there were all sorts of difficulties in the way of procuring the usual comforts for the sick, and up to this time every one, excepting the "Times" commissioner, looked upon a difficulty as an impossibility. It was difficult to get wood, therefore it was impossible to have tables or benches. It was difficult to get iron bedsteads, therefore the men must lie on wooden tressels. It was difficult to get good washing done, so it was left to go on as it best could. Cooking utensils were scarce and dear, so the food must be cooked without: the ladies' hands were crippled by being wholly restricted to the use of the articles furnished by the diet-roll, and all deficiencies were to be supplied by our free gift store, which was small and uncertain.

We continued to buy many things ourselves, kind friends sent us presents also; but we felt the painful uncertainty of this, and we also felt this was not the way in which the army of England should be relieved. Private charity had flowed forth in our emergency, but it should not be overtaxed. The govern-

ment of England ought to be the source
from which it should permanently come.
When Mr. Robertson, the new purveyor in
chief, came into office, this was realised. The
purveying department was soon in a very
different state—in working instead of idling
order. What was required in the hospitals
was procured without delay. First came
iron bedsteads and hair mattresses; next
tables and benches; a sufficiency of tins for
the men's food to be eaten out of.

Other improvements followed. The hospitals assumed a different aspect; now,
indeed, were English soldiers treated as they
deserved. The just complaints began to be
hushed; not that the improvements were
wrought at once or without labour and
difficulty; but Mr. Robertson was a person
determined to overcome obstacles, and who
went simply and straightforwardly about
his business.

It was now we gained possession of the

charcoal brasiers, of which incidental mention has been made. These treasures deserve a more particular description. They are small iron tripods, holding a few pounds of charcoal. They are very difficult to light, and the fire can only be kept alive by being placed in a draught. In the winter, as we have described, we did all our cooking for ten days upon them, but those we then used were borrowed for the emergency. All the ladies and Sisters complained of their not having any fire to go to if they wanted, as so often happened, to make a cup of arrowroot, or warm some wine or water, &c., and it was so tiresome having to send so frequently to the diet kitchen for every little thing: first, it was such a long way off, and in consequence the fetching and carrying took up more than double the time it ought; and secondly, the workers in the diet kitchen found it almost impossible to keep it in order if orderlies and nurses dropped in at all

times asking for every imaginable article, so
that a charcoal brasier for each ward had
long been one of the objects of our ambition,
and now we had but to write requisitions for
them and they were procured immediately.
They were placed in the lobby of each ward,
both that they might have a draught and
also not be an annoyance to the patients.

At night we used our "Etnas." These valuable helps to those who nursed the sick were
brought from England by the ladies—they
were given by kind friends in England as a
last thought for our own comfort should we
be laid up.   Little did the donors imagine
the vicissitudes their Etnas would go through
in an Eastern campaign till they were fairly
battered out.   Before the charcoal brasiers
arrived they were constantly used, but of
course the spirits of wine required to light
them made them rather an expensive luxury.
Still they were our night companions, and
many a little comfort did they enable us to

give to our poor men, to whom they were also an extreme amusement. They would sit up in bed sometimes to watch us boiling an egg or some arrowroot in one of them, saying one to another—

"Ain't that a little beauty, now? It's as handsome a little pot as I've see'd since I left England. I wish we'd had it in the trenches; there were no such things as them up there." Poor fellows, they were easily amused, and it was a real pleasure to us to hear them laugh.

The next good thing that happened was the construction of the ladies' ward-rooms, which was simply dividing off in each ward a small space by means of canvas screens in which were placed two or three chairs and a table; this was a great boon to the ladies, who could thus occasionally take a few minutes' rest, which before they could not obtain except by leaving the hospital and returning home.

The introduction of canvas screens into the wards was a great improvement. Now the delirious, or cholera, or dying patients could be screened off from the others. Before this the sight of the very terrible cases often had a sad effect on their fellow patients.

The fruit season had commenced, and every day the caiques loaded with fruit dashed past the windows of our home. Strawberries were first, through Mr. Stow's kindness, introduced into the wards. Mr. Robertson said the government ought to provide them, and we had as many as we required. The strawberries were very fine, though they did not seem to us to possess the flavour of English ones. There were quantities of melons brought in caiques for sale, but this was a fruit very seldom wanted in the hospital, and the men did not like green figs, of which there were quantities; grapes followed, and they were much appreciated by the fever patients.

Then came the astounding news that the soldiers were to be supplied with pocket-handkerchiefs. Up to this period none were given in the hospitals but from the free-gift store, and it used to be perfectly absurd to hear the ladies begging for them from their superintendent. They were so prized by the men, especially when they were of some bright colour: in fact, with very few exceptions, the men highly appreciated anything which conduced to habits of cleanliness and neatness.

One day a box for me arrived from England, upon opening which I found the contents to be writing paper with views of the war—that published by Messrs. Rock Brothers, Walbrook. A kind friend had sent me a large quantity, and Messrs. Rock themselves added a present of more. Its arrival created a great sensation in the hospital. The ladies and Sisters begged hard for a share. They could not all have it. I gave some to the General Hospital and the rest to the Barrack. It was a great pleasure to distribute them. I spread one of each different view out on the table, and begged the soldiers to make their selection. Everybody who could walk at all crowded round the table. Orderlies and sergeants left their work to have a look, and even the medical officer was attracted by the crowd and came to look and admire. The different views were carried round to the patients in bed. The business of choosing took a long time. Each wanted some scene in which he had formed a part. Some had been with Colonel Chester when he so gallantly led on the 20th; those who had been in the battle of the Alma wished for that; those who had been at Balaclava another; while those again who had fought at Inkermann another. Some had seen General Strangways die, and wanted his last scene; others were less warlike and chose the pretty views of the valley of the Alma before and after the battle, while the comic pictures were not without their share of admirers.

One sergeant was particularly struck by the "Fresh Arrivals"—two young officers fresh from England, in all the pride of new uniforms and polished boots, meeting an old campaigner on a mule who had been out foraging for the mess-table and was bringing home his purchases. The sergeant held this up for the admiration of his comrades, and there was a shout of laughter instantly raised.

I much wish my friend and Messrs. Rock also could have seen the extreme pleasure these gifts were the means of giving—the delight it gave the soldiers to write home on these sheets of paper, or how they were treasured up and compared with each other day after day, and many a tale did the pictures elicit as they brought back more vividly to mind past scenes of Alma and Inkermann, &c. When I wrote home, saying how grateful I was for the present, and how much it had been valued, the same friend sent another packet, which shared the fate of but too many other kind offerings and *was lost.*

Stationery was very much prized; all we had was supplied from our free-gift store, and up to this period had been very scarce, but about this time we had a great deal sent out to us and could supply the demand sufficiently. Now that we had plenty of tables in the ward, we had a store of paper, envelopes, pens, and ink lying on it for all, and in some wards a box to receive the letters, which was emptied on Sunday and Wednesday evenings, and the letters carried home by the ladies and sorted; those to the camp did not need a stamp, those for England were stamped by the chaplain, to whom we gave them. Extraordinary were the directions and spelling that used to occur in these letters—we often wondered how they ever reached their destination. One very common direction to the camp was " Sebastopol, Russia, in Turkey."

There was one great trouble which we began to feel at this time—namely, the conduct of the hired nurses. We had indeed been tried by this from the beginning, and several, as I have mentioned, were sent home for bad conduct; but still the distress around them and the frequent sickness among their own numbers kept some sort of check upon them, and after some had been dismissed for bad conduct and others from sickness only two remained when the new party arrived on April 9th.

The hospital costume in which Miss Stanley's party left England was worn alike by ladies and nurses, which was intended to mark the equality system, but soon after beginning hospital work we found it impossible to continue wearing the same dress as the nurses, and therefore discontinued it. When

the new party arrived, to our dismay we
found that the home authorities had not
thought well to learn experience from those
who had to struggle with difficulties on the
spot; they still held to similarity in dress,
and the ladies and nurses all wore the government costume. When we received them
at Koulali we expressed our surprise and
vexation at the mistake, and our conviction
that the ladies would very soon follow our
example and make a distinction in dress between themselves and the nurses, and the
event proved our expectations correct.

The ladies soon found it was necessary for
their own comfort and for the good of their
work that in every possible way the distinction should be drawn. None but those
who knew it can imagine the wearing
anxiety and the bitter humiliation the
charge of the hired nurses brought upon us,
for it should be remembered that we stood
as a small body of English women in a

foreign country, and that we were so far a community that the act of one disgraced all. After this period, it is true, we had no longer to encounter the hardships some had endured in the winter, but as long as the work in the East lasted so long were there difficulties to be surmounted and trials to be borne of no common character.

On April the 21st, a second party of three ladies and seven nurses joined us. They had travelled under the escort of Mr. Wallace, a clergyman of the Church of England. Immediately on their arrival he informed the lady superintendent that one of the hired nurses had behaved so badly on the passage out she ought to go home; it was fixed she should return by the next ship that left.

Before the party of nurses he had escorted out went to their work, Mr. Wallace wished to address a few words to them, but upon their assembling in the sitting-room one of the number, Mrs. ———, declared she did not

wish to hear it, as she did not intend to stay.
No, the life was " different to what she had
expected "—she had been two days in the
East—and the nurses " were an ungodly set
she could not live among. She was a Christian, and Christians must not live among the
ungodly." Upon inquiry we discovered that
Mrs. ——'s husband was a bandmaster, that
she had come out intending as soon as she
reached the East to leave the service of the
government and join him, but on her arrival
she found he had been sent home, and now
she wished to go back. The superintendent
said she could go if she liked, but she would
not pay her passage home. This quite upset
Mrs. ——'s calculations, as she had reckoned
upon a free passage to England. She became very insolent indeed, and was obliged
to be reminded that, if she did not submit to
the rules of the house, we were in a military
hospital and could call in the assistance of
the authorities. The vision of " arrest "

rather frightened her, she contented herself
with warning us what we might expect when
she did get back to England—she would ex-
pose all our doings.

One of the nurses came to report her
threats in great terror.

"Oh, if you please, ma'am, she does say
such dreadful things that she is a-going to do.
We shall be as good as *massacreed* when she
gets home!"

"Well, never mind," we said, "let her
only go away and get home, and we will see
when the massacre comes."

She left the house on the day the vessel
for England was to sail, went to the British
Consul, and I believe prevailed upon him to
give her a passage to Malta. He probably
did not want her among the British subjects
at Constantinople. The other discharged nurse
was sent to Galata to embark for England,
but contrived to get away from the person in
charge and ran into Constantinople. We

never could trace her afterwards. Such was
the consequence of sending out women of inferior character to such a work of trial and
temptation. We felt it bitterly when we
wished so much that a good example should
be set to the men, and that we should raise and
influence them for the better; it would have
been all undone by these women, while to
them, poor creatures, a military hospital was
the very worst place that could be imagined
—rife with every sort of temptation.

A few weeks only had elapsed since the
departure of the two women I have mentioned, when disgraceful misconduct caused
the dismissal of a third. Ere a passage could
be had for her another was obliged to go,
from her habits of intoxication, and she had
been one most highly recommended; and to
hear her talk you would think she was a very
religious person. These two left together.
The chaplain himself offered to see them on
board, and his task was no light one, for

during the whole caique voyage down the
Bosphorus every sort of abuse and bad language were showered down upon his head.

Our trials were not ended. A similar
case of bad conduct obliged the dismissal of
one whom we had looked upon as one of
our best nurses. Another was found intoxicated in the wards; these two went a
few weeks or two more for the same
reason; and so on till, out of the twenty-one,
in less than eight months we had eleven
left. To our profound astonishment we found
that our sending home so many gave great
umbrage to the authorities at home. They
thought fit to send a reproof, demanding
more particulars of the cases, and evidently
displeased at the number sent back.

They were respectfully reminded that our
superintendent's duties did not include the
reformation of women of loose character and
immoral habits, nor did we imagine the
authorities would require details which were

often too terrible to dwell on. We certainly did expect that the ladies intrusted with the arduous charge of controlling the nurses in our Eastern hospitals were better judges of what class of persons were or were not fit for that work, than those who, safe in English homes, had perhaps never entered an hospital ward at all—certainly never toiled in a military one night and day.

Of the remaining nine two were very unsatisfactory (Mrs. Woodward, who came from Oxford, and had been recommended by Dr. Acland, was quite an exception to what has been said. She was perfectly respectable and trustworthy, and altogether a most valuable person). The other six were respectable and industrious, and under a lady's supervision did very well, but not a single one, except Mrs. Woodward, could be trusted alone. They would give things to favourite patients without the surgeon's leave, or omit to carry out his orders unless they were made to do it.

In ordinary hospitals the nurses constantly do this. I have been told by medical men that, humanly speaking, they have known lives among their patients lost by the nurses' disobedience; but in English hospitals the doctors submit to this—they must have nurses, they can get no better—while in Eastern hospitals the nursing was acknowledged to be an experiment, and it was of the greatest importance strict obedience should be paid to the commands of the surgeons, or we knew not but that it might end in their refusing to accept our aid altogether. It was no easy thing to introduce a new element into the beaten routine of military hospitals, and needed great care, skill, and prudence in those intrusted with its management to do it successfully.

CHAPTER II.

I WILL now speak more fully of what I can
with justice say was the most important part
of our work. When Miss Stanley first entered Koulali Hospital and asked the principal
medical officer what sort of work her nurses
should undertake, the answer at once was
that they should undertake the cooking and
seeing the diets given at proper times.

"It is not the surgical cases," said one of the first-class staff-surgeons, "for which we require your assistance. Their wounds are as well or better dressed by the regular dressers, but it is the medical cases which require watching and feeding, and just that constant care which nurses can and we cannot give, and a large proportion of the present cases require good nursing more than medical skill."

We have described the first formation of the kitchen, its gradual advance from charcoal brasiers to a shed in the yard, and a kitchen in the Sultan's quarters of the hospital. This latter we gave up when we left our apartments there, as it was required for the officers' use. The shed in the barrack-yard was enlarged and improved, and all the extra cooking carried on there, but still it was far from possessing all necessary conveniences.

At the General Hospital for all these

months the Sisters' extra diet cooking had
been done on brasiers; they had no store-
room, and were obliged to keep their free
gifts in their own apartments. In the Barrack Hospital we had a good-size storeroom,
but sadly wanting shelves and other improvements; and there was one great hindrance
which stood in the way of real improvement
in this department : the materials for the
extra diets were drawn daily from the purveyor's store by the orderlies of each ward,
according to their diet roll, and then brought
to the kitchen to be cooked. Great waste
was the natural consequence of this. Small
quantities of sago, rice, arrowroot, were being
cooked for each separate ward, while, if all
were done at once, half the quantity would
be sufficient; and, as I have before mentioned, for any mistake in drawing the
rations, or for any deficiency in the food,
there was no remedy except through private
gifts, which were quite inadequate to the
claims thus made upon them.

When the purveyor-in-chief visited Koulali
this difficulty was laid before him, and he
remedied it at once by giving the lady in
charge of the store-room authority to draw
on the stores and use the materials according
to her own judgment. Finding that the
General Hospital stood greatly in want of a
kitchen and store-room, he furnished them;
two small rooms in the building fronting the
quadrangle were chosen for this purpose,
and the reverend Mother, assisted by Sister
M—— J——, undertook the management.
It was all that was wanting to make the
General Hospital perfect. The two rooms were
beautifully fitted up—the kitchen with oven
and boilers, and brasiers built into the wall
where frying and boiling could go on—the
store room furnished with shelves and
drawers; and when these arrangements
were completed the kitchen was well supplied with cooking utensils, plates, and
dishes, and, what we admired most of all,

small round tins, with a cover attached to it by a chain—these were for the dinners to be served in, and thus kept hot in their travels from the kitchen to the wards.

The store-room was filled with every comfort that could be wished for. Preserved soups of all kinds—we had never been able till now to draw these from the stores—we had in the winter a large quantity of them sent out by Mr. Gamble to Miss Nightingale at Scutari, and she sent on a part to Koulali. They were much prized by the men and also by the then overworked nurses, who at that time were very thankful for anything that enabled them to procure a diet quickly, and Mr. Gamble's preserved meat only requires to be heated and hot water added and it is most excellent soup ready at hand.

" It's the beautifullest thing I ever tasted," said one patient. " That's the stuff to do us good," remarked many others.

Now the store-room shelves had plenty of this soup, and plenty of essence of beef (an invaluable thing in sickness), sago and arrow-root, rice, sugar, gelatine in large quantities, wine and brandy, soda-water, eggs, lemons and oranges; other comforts were afterwards added. The diets were in a very different state; the fowls and chops did not look like the same, and the men said they tasted quite different. Rice-puddings were an important branch in the extra-diet kitchen. It was difficult to make them well, owing to the inferior kind of milk, rice, and eggs. The reverend Mother solved the problem, and as good rice puddings as any one could desire were sent out and gave great satisfaction.

We found it, however, quite impossible to make the puddings properly without using more materials than were allowed us by the diet roll, so that we used our privilege of drawing on the stores to make up the deficiency.

For all the expenditure of the store-room an
account was required to be kept and sent in
to the purveyor's.

Sister M—— J—— was an excellent
accountant. It was a pleasure to look
at her books, and they gained great com-
mendation when they went in to the
purveyor's office to be checked. At the
Barrack Hospital improvements in the extra
diets went on, the kitchen was enlarged and
furnished with fireplaces, additional ovens,
&c. The rice-pudding reform was introduced ; after we saw the beautiful ones sent
out by the Sisters, we were ambitious ours
should be as good, and the superintendent
and the lady in charge of the kitchen begged
the reverend Mother to give them lessons in
this branch of cooking, which she kindly did;
so they went up to the General Hospital and
saw how they were made, and watched the
general routine of the kitchen, and then tried
to copy it below—for the Sisters' long expe-

rience in all matters concerning the care of the poor and sick gave them a great superiority over us, and they were ever ready to show us their method and to enter into our difficulties, and these, in our extra-diet kitchen in Turkey, were not a few. Milk that would turn, eggs the half or more than half the number rotten, the rice filled with dirt, are great obstacles in the construction of puddings, so also are green lemons when you want to make lemonade.

Most of these articles were supplied to the hospital by contract, and when it was a little more difficult than usual to get things—such as milk in the hot weather, or lemons when the season for them was past—they used to send *anything* they could get hold of, and the purveyor would have kept them had we not had permission from the Purveyor-in-Chief to send back inferior articles, for he said the contractors were well paid by Government, and ought and should send articles fit for use.

We soon had excellent rice and rather better milk, but it was impossible to get really good milk anywhere. Lady Stratford de Redcliffe used to send some milk daily to the "Home," from Therapia, which was the best that could be had, and by heating this directly it came in we prevented it from turning, but if this precaution was neglected in the middle of the day it became sour. Good eggs we tried hard for, but could not procure, and were obliged to be content with breaking dozens of rotten ones to arrive at the good. The green lemons we returned, and after some battles with the contractors we got others.

Gelatine was the next difficulty. There was a call for jelly · of course no calves'-feet could be had, so we tried gelatine, one kind of which made it nicely, while the other made it so very thick and bad we could not send it into the wards. It was by no means sufficient just to state this to the purveyor and ask for it to be changed, he thought it would "do very well," so we had to be very resolute to get our way.

The Barrack Hospital extra-diet kitchen had a cook who was a civilian (a good many of whom had been sent out by government). This was a great improvement, as it is difficult to find cooks among the soldiers, and when they are found and practised they are liable—as the orderlies—to be ordered up to their regiment. At the General Hospital, however, Sister M——— J——— had a soldier for a cook who gave her great satisfaction.

The routine of the extra store-rooms was as follows: They were opened at nine in the morning; the nurse who assisted the lady, or Sister, sweeping and dusting, while the lady looked over the total abstract and ladies' requisitions. The former was made by the purveyor's clerk, who examined the diet-rolls of each ward and then made an abstract of the extra diets required of them, and sent

it in to the lady or sister ; the latter were for
such articles as the ladies required extra to
the diet rolls, such as they had verbal permission to give, and for such articles as they
wished to keep in their cupboards for emer-
gencies. They were like the following :—

(No. 50.)   July 19, 1855.

Required for 3 Lower Ward, Koulali Hospital—4 quarts lemonade ; 3 do. milk ; 4 do.
arrowroot ; 2 doz. eggs ; jelly for two ; ½ lb.
of butter ; 2 doz. biscuits.

Miss ——   (Signed)   Sister M—— A——.

Every lady and Sister sent in a requisition.
Except in a case of great emergency they
were only permitted to send once a day for
all they wanted throughout it, as otherwise
irregularity was caused. These requisitions
were then served ; the articles for each
ward were arranged in order, in addition to
the requirements of the diet rolls. Then
the bell was rung and in an instant a group
of orderlies rushed across the barrack-yard

to see who would be in time first and carry
off his extras.   Requisitions from the
medical officers came in at all hours, and
were instantly attended to.

At 12-30 the bell again rang, and the
orderlies assembled to fetch their dinners;
for this purpose they had wooden trays, on
which were counted out the number of fowls,
chops, potatoes, each required, then they returned again for rice pudding, maccaroni
pudding, pints of rice or sago milk; in a
quarter of an hour all were served; then
came diets of sick officers, for among the
large body attached to the hospitals there
were generally one or two on the sick list.
At two the store room was closed till four;
at five the bell summoned the orderlies to
fetch the night drinks—lemonade, barley-
water, or tea, as were ordered; arrowroot or
beef-tea was again made if required.

In the evening the lady in charge wrote
her requisitions on the purveyor's stores for
such articles as she would require for her

store room the next day. On Sundays the
hours were slightly altered, owing to the
arrangement that all persons in the store
room and kitchen should attend Divine service ; but though each had the opportunity
afforded them, the patients were in no ways
neglected.

Most amusing scenes went on at times in
the extra-diet kitchen. The orderlies did
not like the civilian cook, and he returned
the compliment ; they were perpetually
telling tales of each other. Once when Miss
—— was detained from her work for a few
days by illness, she received the following
note from the cook :—

"Madam—I wish to acquaint you about
the malice that is existing among some of
the orderlies towards me, and the other
servants in the kitchen. I believe the cause
to be not having a free intercourse in the
kitchen as formerly, and moreover, an an-
tipathy towards me for doing my duty. If

I have not done my duty to the best of my ability I will refer to your honourable decision. Yesterday evening I had a requisition for six pints of chocolate at 7 P.M., when I was at my room; I was in the act of dressing when the orderly came, I made haste over to the kitchen and the ladies' store was locked, therefore, I could not comply with the requisition. This morning he made a special report to the doctor. Under these circumstances, and with your kind permission, I would like for my welfare and also for the best mode of regulating the kitchen, to have some restrictions. Regarding this, I hope, madam, with my greatest respect, that you will take interest in these few lines. I remain, madam,

" Your humble servant.

" T. R., *Cook*."

There were a good many Greeks also employed in the kitchen (for the labour of fetching water from the extreme end of the barrack-yard required a good many hands, and chopping wood was another piece of heavy work); the Greeks were a great torment, they were perpetually running off, staying away for a day or so and then coming back, and quarrelling and fighting among themselves, and being idle and disobedient. One had to send messages almost every day to the sergeant in charge of the Greeks, "Wanted a Greek."

At last came an Italian named Constantine, he was an old man but worth six Greeks. Always at hand, willing, gentle, and obedient, he picked up a few sentences of English very fast and was very proud of his acquirements. His favourite employment was to help the lady putting out the stores, lifting the heavy weights for her and so on; he was quite honest, but he and cook could not agree and there were dreadful battles. Cook complained so of his disobedience in the kitchen that Miss —— was forced to speak to him;

and it was very absurd, as she could not speak either Greek or Italian, and had to express her displeasure by using the little English Constantine knew and by signs. Constantine understood quite well, and made a vehement defence; he danced about the room, and, with many gesticulations, gave her to understand that "Monsieur Cook" was so unreasonable, he wanted Constantine to be in the kitchen when he was helping madame in the store room, and that he could not be in two places at once, and Monsieur Cook was so rough he called out so loud and was not quiet like madame. However, the reproof did good, and the kitchen was more peaceable.

Monsieur Soyer paid a visit to Koulali before the improvements in the extra-diet kitchen had taken place. He offered to show a better way of making the hospital tea, *i. e.*, that issued from the large general kitchen for all the diets. There was room

for improvement, for it was the most
wretched stuff possible. Monsieur Soyer's
was much better, and yet he made it, he
said, with exactly the same proportions as
before. I do not think his improvements
were attended to at the kitchen, but as it
did not come within our province I cannot
be sure.

Monsieur Soyer made his tea in the little
kitchen outside the Convalescent Hospital.
The medical officers and the ladies came to
taste it, and it was an amusing scene : the
group outside tasting the tea, the tiny
kitchen, which just held Monsieur Soyer and
his assistants, and the patients of the Convalescent Hospital looking on and wondering
what was going to happen to their tea that
night.

CHAPTER III.

THE routine of the hospital was often
interrupted by the arrival of sick, who came
in numbers varying from 50 to 100. We
seldom had more than a few hours' notice,
and often not that. Sometimes it was not
till the steamer was alongside the quay that
we knew they were coming; this arose from
all the sick from the camp being sent to

Scutari first and the steamer coming back from thence to Koulali.   When they arrived there was a general commotion ; the principal medical officer, the commandant, and most of the medical staff went down to the quay to receive them and see them carefully carried up.   Orderlies ran hither and thither, ward-masters and nurses were in a bustle getting beds prepared.   The kitchen staff was hard at work to get coppers full of hot water, and fires lighted in readiness for the doctor's orders.   Ladies and Sisters looking after the clean linen.

A different scene it was truly from that which used to be presented a few months back, when the poor sufferers came in and no beds were ready and no clean linen, and no nurses to attend and watch by them.   A blessed change indeed it was.

There was a division made of the sick, part going to the Barrack and part going to the General hospitals. All who were able walked, the rest were borne on stretchers. As soon as the sick were in their beds requisitions began to pour in. One ward ordered beef tea, another negus, a third *good* tea. The orderly officer for the day was in great request as he must sign the requisitions, or give the Sisters and ladies verbal orders from which they might write their own requisitions.

Very touching incidents often occurred among the sick just come in; they were so astonished to find so many comforts ready, and so many hands to minister to them. The quantity of clean linen was a great wonderment; they said they had more here in a week than in the camp for months together.

The poor Irish soldiers were much charmed at the sight of the nuns—" Our own Sisters," they would fondly say.

I remember one poor man brought in who was a Roman Catholic; he was so ill he could not speak, could neither ask for temporal comfort or spiritual consolation, but he looked up into the face of the Sister who was attending on him, and perceiving the crucifix hanging from her girdle eagerly seized it with his dying grasp and pressed it fervently to his lips.

The national spirit of the Irish was very strong ; it was pleasing to see their reverence and affection for their priests and the nuns. The Irish orderlies used to be delighted beyond measure to be allowed to wait on the Catholic chaplain; nothing was so great a treat as to be doing something for " his riverence."

There were amusing scenes sometimes with Irish sailors. There was a wharf just below Koulali, where steamers often came to coal ; once or twice the crews were principally Irish. The sailors had leave to go on shore, and dispersed themselves about the country ; they went through the hospital wards, evidently delighted at the comfortable appearance of the men. They looked at and admired everything; but when they met their countrywomen—the Sisters of Mercy—in the barrack-yard they were quite over-joyed. When they found that they lived at the General Hospital they poured up the hill in troops to visit them and attend their chapel. Many who had not attended to their religious duties for years were persuaded to do so now. They did not forget the ladies either, but were overheard one night on the quay to be talking the matter over, and saying, *however* those ladies could have come out all this way with nobody to take care of them was past *their* conception.

Butter was a great treat to our men; before the arrival of the new Purveyor-in-chief the bread was so dry and sour that it was difficult even for those in health to force it down unless very hungry. No butter was at that time given on the diet roll. We asked the leave of the medical officers to give it to our patients. This was granted, and we were enabled to obtain it through the kindness of friends in England, who sent us money for this and such-like purposes. It will gratify them to know that many and many a poor fellow had a comfortable meal through their consideration.

We are glad to take this opportunity of thanking them for the warm, affectionate sympathy and ready help they so often afforded us, not only in sending us money and other presents but for the personal trouble they took in the matter. We had but to write to England and say we wanted such and such a thing and it was sent by the first opportunity, and not only this but we often received letters begging us to write and say what things would be useful. Little school children sent us money—small sums they had saved, and wished to be sent to the " ladies who nursed the sick soldiers."

Could these friends have seen the glistening eyes with which the poor men listened

to the account of their kindness, and have
heard their hearty " God bless them—God
bless them !" they would have been more
than rewarded. It would have pleased them
to have gone round our wards with us at
tea-time, accompanied by our butter-bowl,
and have seen the grateful look of each patient as he received his small portion, and
have heard his exclamation, " Why, here's
actually a bit of butter—that *is* nice and
homelike !" Many would keep half their portions till next morning's breakfast. It certainly was very unlike English butter, and
we sometimes wondered how they could eat
it with such evident enjoyment ; but long
months of hardship and almost starvation
had taught them to be easily satisfied with
what many in England would have grumbled
at. Our means of procuring them this comfort of course soon came to an end. It was
not fair to give butter in one ward and not
in another, and one £3 after another was

quickly spent in providing a whole hospital
with butter, even once or twice a week, as it
cost from 3s. to 4s. a pound.   4s. we always
paid for it when we bought it at the canteens,
but we could procure it at 3s. if we bought
casks of £2 or £3 value at Constantinople.

When Mr. Robertson came he ordered
butter to be had in the stores, and we drew
it upon requisition, and gave it when we
thought the men really needed it.   Next we
happened to be complaining to one of the
officer's wives of the sour bread furnished to
the hospital, which also came to our own
table.   She said it was very strange, their
bread was beautiful, as good or better than
English.   We found this arose from the
officers' rations being drawn from the commissariat department, while ours came, like
the patients', from the purveying, and that
these two departments had separate contractors for bread.   Upon this being represented to the purveyor-in-chief he changed

the bread contract at Midsummer, and from that time the hospital was supplied with excellent bread, the contractor being Mr. Hamelin, the Armenian Minister at Bebek. From his bakery long previous to this we procured biscuits which were very good. They were twelve piastres the ock (an ock is about two and a half pounds), so that they are much cheaper as well as better than any we could have procured in the French shops at Pera.

We spent a good deal of our free-gift money in purchasing them, for we often found men who were very weak could eat biscuits when they could not swallow or digest bread. Eventually biscuits, like every other imaginable comfort, could be freely drawn from Government stores.

The bad washing, and consequent deficiency in the linen department, had been severely felt from the first, but there was no remedy. At Scutari the washing, we heard, was now well regulated, being done on the spot by means of washing machines, but this could not be done at Koulali, as there was no building which could be made into a washhouse ; all that could be done was to place the linen stores under the charge of the Sisters and ladies. It was a point on which Mr. Robertson was very anxious. He had rooms fitted up for this purpose at both hospitals ; at the upper one it was under the charge of Sister J——— M———, who began hers first, and it was conducted in beautiful order.

The linen stores of the Lower Hospital was under Miss ———, and nurses assisted in both stores.

The care of the linen stores was a very laborious work. The lady superintendent, in addition to her numerous duties, spent much of her time in those at the Barrack Hospital ; she kept the accounts, and brought it by degrees into perfect shape and order.

The washing was sent across to Bebek, where it was contracted for by the Protestant Armenian Minister there.   It was executed by Greeks, who sometimes thought fit to work and sometimes not, so that often the washing was in arrear. A great quantity of linen always had to be returned to be washed again—a momentary dip in the water evidently having been the extent of labour bestowed upon it.

When the washing came over it was taken to the sergeants, who had charge of the soiled linen (this department being of course under sergeant and orderlies), clean linen was then sent to the linen stores upon requisition. The ladies and Sisters who worked at the linen stores spent their whole daytime there, only leaving it for meals and evening recreations. Twice a-week they received the clean linen, and after sending back the badly washed they proceeded to sort the articles, then followed the folding, and lastly the mending.

Twice a-week the ladies and Sisters of the respective wards sent in their requisitions, the ladies at the linen store served these, put the different articles in bundles for the wards, and then the orderlies fetched them. The Sisters and ladies had in their wards linen cupboards (under lock and key), where they kept a small quantity of linen ready in case of sudden illness or fresh cases coming in.

It took a long time before the linen stores were arranged in a satisfactory manner, but we at length succeeded, and had now the pleasure of knowing that there was no comfort required in sickness which was not supplied to the British soldier. He had the best medical skill and suitable attention, food as good as could be had in Turkey, and linen in as great a quantity as in the hospitals at home.

The work in the linen stores was so very arduous that the other ladies, when their work in the wards was lighter than usual, often dropped in to lend their assistance towards reducing the interminable mending.

CHAPTER IV.

The Free Gift Store—Uselessness of a large portion of
what was sent out—Small-tooth combs—Formation
of a separate establishment for the Free Gift Store—
Unpacking of the boxes—Their contents—The principal use of the free gifts—Departure of invalids for
England—Farewells—Kits for the convalescents—
A soldier's petition—Soldiers' wives—An unfortunate accident.

THE Free Gift Store has often been re-
ferred to; it was the store supplied by the
gifts of the people of England, who gener-
ously and promptly sent them out to their
suffering army; and although much disappointment has, I know, been experienced by
many on hearing that numbers of these packages never reached their destination, yet it
will be a satisfaction to many to learn the
benefit given by that portion which did
arrive.

The free gifts had to be carefully sorted, for often a good many useless things were sent out. Some portion of the free gifts sent to Scutari was forwarded to Koulali. Others were sent straight to us, and some we purchased with money sent out from England. Small-tooth combs we bought in great numbers when the hospital was crowded, for they were much needed. An old Turk used to sit at the hospital gate with a stall of trifles, and had some small-tooth combs—he looked so surprised when we broke his stall of them.

At first we had no separate store to keep our free gifts in, but they were kept in one of the government stores, and under charge of the sergeant who had charge of the first. He was an amusing individual, very unlike the soldiers in general, and so very grand that he thought it rather a condescension on his part to attend to us.

After a time a shed in the barrack yard, that had been a canteen, was given up to our

use, and was by the engineer officer made
into a nice little building in three compart-
ments:—First, the superintendent's room;
second, the Free Gift Store; third, for
packing cases, &c. As soon as we could
carry our free gifts into this store, the superintendent arranged them all in order on the
shelves, with which the room was furnished.
Sometimes it looked quite full, but never
remained so for long together; a party of
invalids ordered home soon made a hole in
it. This store was under the Lady superintendent's charge. She saw the things un-
packed and arranged, and received the
requisitions signed by the ladies and Sisters
for what they considered their men needed
before going to England or to the camp.

When Miss Stanley was lady superintendent she divided the gifts among the
ladies in charge of the wards, who distributed them according to their own judgment, and this plan was followed out after

Miss Stanley's departure. The unpacking of the boxes was often quite affecting. Many a wish was expressed that the kind contributors could see the pleasure their gifts gave. There were packages of lint, of mittens, of comforters made up and enclosed as the gift of the poor. There was one packet of sugar-candy, with a note in a large round hand, "For the sick soldiers, from a little girl." Another "from a little German girl." Quantities of pocket handkerchiefs were also sent; flannels, Jerseys, socks, night-caps; some crimson pocket handkerchiefs gave great delight, cotton shirts were also valued.

We found the free gifts principally useful as affording us the means of giving necessaries to the men going to England, for they would otherwise have taken that voyage often without a change of linen or any warm clothing. The men who came down in the winter and spring had usually lost their kits in the camp, and so were quite destitute. Long afterwards, when the men did bring their kits down with them, we always enquired what was deficient in them. After the quarter-master had given what he thought requisite, we then gave them articles from our store; so that it was always busy work when the men were going home, for another rule was not to give the things till just as they were going away, that there might be no temptation thrown in their way to sell their clothes for drink. Consequently all had to be done in a few hours. The ladies wrote their list of what the men wanted, and the superintendent gave them out, and as soon as we had given them they went on board.

The scene at these times was always very interesting. Groups of poor fellows in each ward just risen from their beds and dressed in the uniform of the different regiments, packing up their kits, and reiterating their thanks for the clothes they had just received.

Orderlies running about trying to get the invalids' dinners a little sooner than the usual hour, that the invalids might have a good meal before starting. Comrades who had fought together on the field of battle, or suffered side by side in the trenches before Sebastopol, wishing each other good-bye, those who were left behind sending messages to their friends in England. Chaplains giving away Bibles and prayer books, and as a last kind thought very often finding a quantity of tobacco for them to smoke on the voyage. Sisters and ladies having a last word with those whom they had long tended, and whom in all human probability they would never meet again in this world, many of these with tears in their eyes loading them with blessings, and earnestly promising (what they well knew would more than compensate for any trouble they might have taken) that they would be different men henceforth to what they had been before they came into the hospital.

And now the order is loudly given at the entrance of each ward, "The invalids for England to proceed to the shore," and they slowly depart—orderlies carrying the kits of those who are too weak to do so themselves, and some of the wounded and incurable being taken down on stretchers. They all pass down the barrack yard and through the main guard entrance, which is crowded with doctors and officers. One of these accompanies the invalids as far as Scutari, where they embark in a larger vessel for England— and now the little steamer is ready—the poor fellows are all on board, and we watch them depart with a silent prayer for their safe arrival in old England.

On Mondays and Thursdays patients were discharged from the convalescent hospital to proceed to Scutari, from thence to go to the camp, and what we considered deficient in their kits were made up from the Free Gift Store, so that it had enough to do to supply all these demands. Sometimes it did get alarmingly low, but somehow, by hook or by crook, it got up again, and we always had enough to give. The men were so grateful for these gifts, and so pleased with them. An amusing letter was sent to one of us once which I insert—the cotton shirts the writer speaks of had been given but not the rest of the free gifts, and he was very much afraid none were coming.

" Miss ——,—Please if in your power to let me have the following articles, *viz.*, one pair of slippers, for my feet are very sore ; one red scarf; one night-cap ; one pocket-handkerchief.

" N.B.—None of the above have I received, though you have supplied me well with clean linen for the voyage, for which I sincerely thank you, and your kindness to me and to every one in the ward shall never be forgotten or neglected in the prayers of your humble servant,

" CORPORAL G——.

" A flannel shirt and a pair of drawers

would be most welcome indeed, for I have
one of each, and I'd like to have a change.

" G——."

Occasionally soldiers' wives would be
leaving with the invalids.   There were,
however, very few of these women at
Koulali ; the greater number of them were
at Scutari, where they received much kindness and assistance from Lady Alicia Black-
wood when they left for England, if they
were deserving cases.   They also received
clothes for the voyage.   She commissioned
Sister Anne to undertake the business for
her at Koulali.   They were often in great
distress for clothes, both for themselves and
children, and clothes were far more valuable
to them than money, owing to the great
difficulty of procuring and high price to be
given for them in Pera.   Lady Napier was
also very kind in sending clothes to Sister
Anne to distribute among them.

One poor woman, who washed for the officers, had fallen asleep late one night in the wash-house, and her clothes caught fire. She was frightfully burnt, and was carried to a room over one of the wards where doctors and nurses attended to her. For eight or nine months she lay there unable to move, her husband also in the hospital. They were both invalided home, but she was not able to undertake the voyage, and when we left Koulali she was still there.

CHAPTER V.

THERE are several pretty walks around
Koulali, but we did not often take them as

we were afraid to be far out of call of the
sentries ; our usual walks were to the Turkish cemetery, or the Sultan's kiosk.   The
cemetery was on a hill a little beyond the
General Hospital ; it is a grove of cypresses
interspersed with white marble tombstones.
The immense extent of these cemeteries
arose from the custom of planting a cypress
at each grave.   This custom is not now so
general, the Turks never place more than
one body in a grave.

The Turkish name for Koulali is Kulleh
Baghdshessi, or the garden of the tower.
There is a legend attached to it.   Sultan
Selim the 1st was so enraged against his
son Suleikam that he commanded his vizier
to have him strangled.   The vizier, however,
risked his own life to save that of the prince.
He confined him for three years in a tower
at Koulali.   Selim one day repented himself
of his cruelty—for he had no other children
—and then the vizier thought fit to confess

his disobedience. Selim was succeeded by
Suleiman, who pulled down the tower and
planted a beautiful garden and fountain on
the spot of his captivity.

The Sultan's kiosk is built on the point of
the highest hill above Koulali. It was such
labour to climb it that we seldom went,
but when we did gain the summit the view
was magnificent, for we could see miles of
the Bosphorus and the Sea of Marmora.

The next village to Koulali is Candilee,
and it is a lovely spot; its ancient name
meant stream-girt, from the strength of the
current which washes its banks, but now it
is called Candilee, *i. e.*, hung with lanterns.
It is impossible to describe the exquisite
beauty of the views from Candilee. Several
English gentlemen have country houses here;
from one we visited we saw plainly the
Black Sea, the Sea of Marmora, almost the
whole extent of the Bosphorus, hills, and palaces, and groves without number—Europe

and Asia at one glance. The advantage of
living on the summit of these hills is their
extreme coolness—the only drawback being
the labour of ascending them.

Opposite Candilee, on the European coast,
is the village of Bebek, with its lovely bay,
a favourite resort of Europeans. Here are
several American families, and also French and
German. Here are also two colleges—one a
French Catholic, under the order of Lazar-
ist Fathers, the other a Protestant Armenian, under the care of an Armenian gentleman. There is also a small convent and *enfants trouvés*, belonging to the *Sœurs de la
Charité*. We visited these three institutions ;
the first contained about 500 boys, who were
all dressed like French soldiers, and among
their other studies military exercises are di-
ligently learned, a French soldier being
their instructor. Boys of every nation are
there—Turks even send their sons, so that
the facility of acquiring languages is very

great. We counted ten that are spoken in the house.

We were most courteously received by the Superior, and conducted over the college. We saw the library and the laboratory, and the boys at their gymnastics, and heard their singing in the little chapel. The music was an improvement on the general character of French music in the East, but the chapel was so much too small for the large body of voice accompanied by an organ, that we could hardly judge of its merits. We enquired whether the Turkish boys attend the chapel. The answer was "seldom." It was entirely voluntary; if they wished for religious instruction they had it, but they were not forced to hear it.

The superior himself conducted us to the *Maison de Saint Joseph* close by, belonging to the Sisters of Charity; they are sent from the convent at Galata. Their house is for sick children and the *enfants trouvés*, on a

very small scale, however, in comparison to
the well-known institutions of Paris.

Here again the amalgamation of different
nations struck us,—a *Sœur* was standing at
a window holding in her arms a dark-eyed
Italian baby, a fair-haired German child was
climbing up her knee, while a little sickly-
looking *Russian* sat beside her. Groups of
other little ones, some suffering from sickness
and others the lonely and forsaken, played
about the room. Four Sisters were in charge
of them, gathering, as these sweet Sisters
ever do, the most desolate and afflicted of
God's creatures into their loving care. The
college and Sister's house stand in a lovely
situation, half-way up the hill, looking down
on the Bosphorus.

We visited the Protestant Armenian
College, and were most kindly received by
the principal and his family. We were
conducted over the college library, dor-
mitories, &c., but it being the recess we did

not see the pupils. The college is intended for young Armenian men belonging to the sect of Protestant Armenians. Mr. H——, the principal, kindly invited us to spend an evening with his family, and walk to see the French camp, then lying about a mile from their residence—the sight, he said, was worth looking at.

We accepted the invitation, and afterwards spent a pleasant evening at Bebek, but in the interim cholera had broken out in the French camp, which had been moved elsewhere; we returned home that evening by moonlight and the Bosphorus looked like a plain of silver light. Clearly in the brilliance stood out the hills and surrounding houses; now and then a caique darted past us like a bird, so swiftly did it go; in the distance was the city, looking dim and shadowy; the current was with us and our row took us only ten minutes, when against the current we were half an hour or more coming across.

About this time we had occasion to visit
Therapia, and some of us who had there spent
the first six weeks of our lives in the East were
desirous of seeing it in its summer aspect; on
our journey up the Bosphorus we passed the
village of Yenikoi, which was full of huts
containing the sick of the Sardinian army.
A great many Greeks live at Yenikoi, for
here begins the part of the river where the
Christians are allowed to build country
houses.   When we reached Therapia a
change was indeed apparent.   The Sultan's
palace was converted into a convalescent
hospital for the British, and was in beautiful order.   We walked in the extensive
grounds, under the shade of the magnificent
trees which must form such a delightful walk
for the invalids.

After visiting our kind friends at the
hospital we walked through the town along
the quay to the embassy gardens—they were
indeed lovely—the lilac Judas trees and

acacia in full blossom, large white arums geraniums and myrtles grew in profusion, while the garden of Lord Napier's house was a wilderness of China roses. We climbed the steep path up to the flag-staff and gazed on the once familiar view so very lovely now in the summer brightness.

The sweet waters of Asia are situated just below Anatoli Hissar, and thus exactly opposite to Humeli Hissar; these two fortresses are called by Europeans the Castles of Europe and Asia, being built as defences for the narrowest part of the Bosphorus. Here Darius crossed with his army, with horses, elephants, and camels, on his expedition against the Scythians. On a stone pillar on each shore were inscribed the names of the nations who crossed with him. Here was also the rock cut into the form of a throne, where Darius sat and contemplated the march of his army from Asia to Europe; to the building of the walls of this fortress were applied the pillars and altars of the Church of St. Michael which had been built at Koulali. The Castle of Europe was built 1451, two years before the Ottoman conquest of Constantinople; the Castle of Asia had been erected some time previously. This latter was once called Guzel Hissar, *i. e.*, the beautiful castle; but terrible tales would be told could those ruined walls find a tongue, for afterwards they named the beautiful castle the Black Tower, for many hundreds here met their death from torture and cruelty. Strange that in a spot which God has made fair beyond the power of language to describe, man has delighted in the cry of agony. Many other armies have followed the example of Darius, and crossed the Bosphorus at this point,—Persians, Goths, Latins, and Turks.

The Castle of Asia is entirely in ruins, but the Castle of Europe is still standing. It was built intending to form the Turkish characters of M H M D, which make the name of the founder Mahomet II.

After rowing three miles down we came to the narrow creek leading to the sweet waters, about a quarter of a mile in length; the name of this creek or small river is Göhsu, *i. e.*, the heavenly water. It is considered the most lovely spot in Asia—the water has rather a sweet taste, from whence has arisen its name—it is always called sweet waters. Each side is hung with trees bending down to the water's edge. At the end of the creek we generally landed and walked in the green fields beyond. The pleasure of this excursion principally consisted in our being able to say, we could fancy ourselves in England. The scenery rather reminded some of us of that in the south of Devonshire.

On Friday (the Turkish Sabbath), the valley of the sweet waters is the favourite rendezvous of the Turkish ladies. They

assemble beneath some large green trees in a
field on the banks of the sweet waters; close
by rises a new palace the Sultan is building.
The windings of the Bosphorus, and its hills
crowned with kiosks, and its banks crowded
with houses can be seen for some distance as
one stands in the valley of sweet waters.
The white and ivy covered towers of the
Castle of Europe form a striking picture in
the landscape; near the banks is a marble
fountain, richly ornamented with carving;
but on a Friday the scene in the valley
itself almost distracted one's attention from
the landscape.

Under the trees are spread carpets and
cushions of various colours, upon these re-
cline the Turkish ladies sitting in groups
clothed in dresses of every bright hue—
green, blue, red, pink, yellow, orange,
violet, &c. Some are smoking, some are
drinking coffee out of their tiny cups, some
buying sweatmeats and toys—vendors of

these are straying about in all directions—children in their quaint Turkish dresses, miniatures of their elders, are playing about—heavy Turkish carriages containing the Sultanas and other ladies of high rank, drive slowly round the field—Greek ladies and gentlemen, and children, and French ditto. Here and there an Albanian diversifies the scene.

We here observed one of the most beautiful women we had seen since we came to Turkey. She was seated on a pile of cushions under a large tree, and was dressed in a pale lavender cashmere, a white yashmac, feridjee, and yellow gloves—these latter articles being only worn by ladies of high rank; and from the number of slaves which surrounded her we guessed her to be a person of distinction. It was her perfect grace of attitude which struck us; for although one may often see a beautiful face in Turkey, it is generally accompanied by an awkward, ungraceful

carriage. But like an heroine of some old
Eastern tale sat the lady of whom we speak.
How we longed for an artist's pencil to
draw her picture, and the panorama around.
Could it be real, or were we looking through
a kaleidescope ?

As it grew dark the ladies entered their
carriages or caiques to return home, and we
too sought ours, and were soon at home, for
the current bore us swiftly along.

The currents of the Bosphorus are very
strong, and on some days, without visible
reason, will be much more so than on others.
Immediately before our house was one of the
strongest ; it often drove quite a large ship
back—indeed the larger ships and vessels
seemed more under its influence than the
small boats ; for they, after two or three vain
attempts to stem it, would go cautiously into
the middle of the stream, and so avoid some
of its fury. But the ships were helpless
without the aid of a steamer; they turned

round and round, and we often expected to
see the yards come through our windows.
In fact it once happened that a ship did
injure one of the rooms, and another knocked
down part of our garden wall.

On one occasion, too, we witnessed from
our windows a sad accident. A poor man,
owing to a concussion between two boats,
fell into the seething waters, his rescue was
impossible, and he was drowned before our
eyes. This current is called shcitan akindi-
si, or devil's current, and to it there belongs
a legend. A sultana in her caique was once
proceeding down the Bosphorus when she
met a number of persons going to worship
in a Christian church, upon which she ordered
the church to be pulled down. On her
return her caique was seized by the current
and upset, but all the attendants and boat-
men were saved, the Sultana only was
lost. Almost every spot in Turkey has some
old legend attached to it.

One of our favourite expeditions was to the lovely gardens of Bebek. They belonged to the Sultan's chief physician, who very kindly threw them open to the English or French. It was refreshing after a long hot day's work in the hospital, to row across and wander among the orange and citron groves and sit under the shadowy trees, while the air around was laden with the sweet scent of innumerable flowers, the birds singing over our heads the only sound, and everything above, beneath, and around bright with beauty. We could have fancied ourselves in fairy land,—"And the fire-flies glance in the myrtle boughs,"—completed the dream-like loveliness of the whole scene.

The gardens are most beautifully laid out, terrace above terrace, and bower succeeding bower, and many a winding path, forming gradual ascents to the hills immediately above, from whence can be seen as usual an extensive and beautiful view.

Our last visit to these gardens was late in the autumn, one evening at sun-setting; their aspect changed, but the golden tints on tree and bower contrasting with the deep crimson of the autumn roses rather increased than diminished their beauty. One night too we visited them by moonlight, and the scene was one of un-earthly beauty. Bebek was so easy of access from Koulali that we often went across, and the nurses used to be very fond of visiting these gardens, and we were glad to find occasional amusement for them.

It is said there is an old Turkish super-stition that no man dies while he is building a house, and that this is one reason why the Sultans of Turkey have built such innumera-ble palaces; no one content with those raised by his ancestors, but each new sovereign commencing some new work. Up to this

time, however, all the royal buildings have
been made of wood, believing that it was
good enough for man, while stone was only
fit for the temples of God. But Abdul
Medjid has broken through the custom, and
is building for himself a magnificent palace
of marble immediately above Constantinople.
It is called Dolmabaghdshah, or the filled-up
garden. It forms one of the finest objects in
the scenery of the Bosphorus; its extent is
very great. Along the whole front runs a
marble terrace, bordered with pillars and
grating of finely-wrought iron, richly gilded.

The principal gateway is in the centre of
this terrace, and there are several side en-
trances from all of which lead flights of
marble steps, whose foundation rests in the
water.

There used to be even more difficulty in
the Franks gaining admission to view this
palace than in other Turkish buildings, but
those times are passed, and the allies have

broken down the barrier—nothing more is needed than to go under the escort of an officer whose uniform and sword, accompanied of course with "backshish," throw open the doors.

We disembarked at one side entrance, the grand entrance being reserved expressly for the Sultan. We entered the grand hall in which the Sultan holds his audience. The *coup d'œil* was grand—rich gilding, fresco painting, and marble pillars presented a splendid scene. But the first effect was almost all; and with a nearer view the illusion vanishes, and the true Turkish architecture is clearly to be discerned, for general effect, with total absence of good detail, is its characteristic. The marble pillars were but painted wood! while a close view into every detail gave such an impression of rudeness and imperfection that we soon gave up the examination.

We ascended to the upper apartments, and

were struck by another hall surmounted with a dome of ruby glass. The effect of this we liked exceedingly; the white marble of this hall was neither gilded nor painted, but only lit up with this deep glow. The effect was dazzling, reminding one rather of the hall in Aladdin's palace than any building belonging to this "work-a-day world." Almost all the innumerable apartments of the Sultan, for there are hundreds of them, are ornamented with fresco paintings. The principal devices are of flowers, which gives a great sameness; the reason of this is that the Koran forbids the representation of any human or animal life, bestowing on those who disobey the curse of hereafter giving an account of the souls of those whose bodies they had thus dared to represent on earth. Another disappointment was, with the exception of the two halls, the extreme smallness of the regal apartments. Instead of constructing extensive ones, the space is broken up in continuous small rooms opening into each other.

The Imperial Hareém is separated from the other part of the palace by a corridor and garden. Upon entering we were instantly struck with the extreme contrast to the splendour of the other part of the palace. With a few exceptions, the rooms were perfectly plain, and the bed-rooms resembled those of a modern London house.

The Sultana's drawing-room was, however, very prettily ornamented, and hung with innumerable glass chandeliers. We observed the introduction of a number of chairs in addition to the universal divan. One room, apparently set apart for study, was papered with deep crimson, the curtains and furniture of the same colour, chairs richly gilt; bureau and escritoire of polished wood were placed in different parts of the room; a pair of small globes stood on the table—all this evidently of Parisian workmanship.

But the gem of the palace is yet to be described—this was the Sultan's bath. We passed through a series of marble cooling rooms till we reached the bath. It is entirely of pale yellow alabaster, a kind rarely seen and difficult to procure. The roof was, of course, pierced to allow the vapour to escape; the sculpture is magnificent, and executed with the most delicate precision. There are several fountains, which, when the bath is heated, will pour forth rose-water.

The palace is not yet completed, though many of the rooms are completely furnished. The Sultan comes here daily at two p.m. to receive his officers of state; after this hour, therefore, no visitors are admitted. The Turk who conducted us over the palace seemed anxious to impress upon our minds the awful consequence of incurring the displeasure of the Sultan by speaking too loud or making the slightest sound. Upon our entrance he declared we must take off our shoes; we did not feel inclined to walk over all the marble floors without them, and resisted; and, after some discussion, additional backshish prevailed on him to waive the point as regarded the ladies, and he only insisted that the gentlemen of the party should slip huge Turkish slippers over their boots.

He walked first on tip-toe, putting his finger to his mouth, and when we talked or laughed he drew his arm across his throat, saying, "Sooltan, Sooltan," intimating that we had better take care of our heads. He seemed much entertained, though somewhat aghast at our extreme indifference to this warning. He evidently thought our continued laughing and talking a proof of wonderful courage; in fact, it so much excited his admiration, that on parting from him at the door of the palace, he made us understand that he would have no objection to cicerone us on a future occasion.

The garden was too formal and shrubless
to attract our attention; it is laid out in
numerous flower beds. The view from the
windows is, as usual from buildings on the
Bosphorus, exceedingly magnificent.

CHAPTER VI.

PAPAFEE, our strange interpreter, who has
been already mentioned, did not improve as
time went on. We were often on the point

of dismissing him and seeking another servant, but he used to go to Lady Stratford
and talk her over, and, much to our astonishment, she expressed her wish that he should
remain.   He was a real annoyance, and, had
it not been for the sake of his wife, who was
a great comfort in sickness, we must have
insisted on his removal.   He used to scold
us, tell falsehoods, offer his advice when quite
unasked and unwished for; sometimes refused to do what he was told, and, when he
did condescend to be obedient, let us fully
understand that he was good enough to bend
his superior judgment to our want of sense.

If we seriously offended him he would
threaten to write to England and report us
to government.   His whole conduct was so
utterly absurd that we had many a laugh
about it, and had these scenes only occurred
now and then they would have been rather
an amusement than otherwise, but with our
various occupations and many calls, both on

time and patience, this could not always be the case.

Papafée's wife was a little German woman, extremely gentle and quiet, and was the very opposite of her husband, who used to scold her loudly and severely if she the least displeased him, which was not a difficult matter to accomplish, and one of daily occurrence, though it was generally quite unintentional on her part; added to which she was much out of health, and needed kindness and attention. One of our ladies remonstrated with him on the subject.

" It ees very easy for you to talk," replied he; "you are an English lady, and it comes natural to you to be verie gentle and quiet, and you do say 'pleese do thees, and pleese do that,' but as for me I am of a deeferent deesposition. I was born in a deeferent contree, and am verie passionate, and beesides I can reed the Bible, and I do see there that the wife is to obey her husband, and that he ees to rule over her."

"Yes," replied the lady, "but the Bible also says husbands are to be kind to their wives."

"Oh, vell," said he, "so I am—I am verie kind indeed to her. You should jist see what beauteeful dresses I do give her. I do assure you they are verie fine. In my own contree I am quite a gentleman, and I could have married any lady I chose. My wife was verie luckee to get mee for her husband." This was an opinion in which no one shared, however, not even poor Rosalie herself.

Happily for us we heard one day that our interpreter was wanted by a gentleman proceeding to the camp, who would give him better pay than he received from us. We were only too glad to release him, and he accordingly went up to the front, leaving his wife and child with us till he could make arrangements for them to join him.

Two months passed away, when one even-

ing, as we were all sitting at tea in our
dining-room, which opened to the garden, we
saw coming down the path a tall, distin-
guished-looking officer. We wondered who
it could be. To our surprise, instead of call-
ing the servant he walked straight into the
room, *sans cérémonie.* I thought he was some
official come on important business from
General Storks. Walking up to the head of
the table, and making a low bow to our
superintendent, he "hoped we were all well,
and was glad to see us again," and not till
then did we recognise our former plague and
interpreter, Monsieur Papafée.

He then informed us that he was doing
very well in the camp, and had come to fetch
his wife and child, thinking Madame Papafée
would turn a penny up there cooking for the
officers. His appearance altogether was
really so striking and elegant that we asked
one another was it possible he had ever stood
behind our chairs in white shirt sleeves and

apron, or that we had ever asked him for a
plate?

The next day one of us, returning from the
hospital, saw a lady and gentleman walking
arm-in-arm on the quay, followed by a
servant carrying a child. On approaching
them it proved to be Monsieur and Madame
Papafée, whom we imagined he had ordered
to deck herself for the occasion in one of the
beautiful dresses he had once alluded to, as
proving his devoted affection to the poor
little woman. He made a polite bow as the
lady passed. They went to the camp, but
not long afterwards, when walking in Pera,
one of us was suddenly accosted by Papafée,
who said he had left his situation at Sebastopol because, although it was very nice to
be well paid, it was anything but agreeable
to have a cannon ball coming into one's tent
at all hours of the day or night; and a shell
having burst in close proximity to his abode
he had forthwith packed up and departed,

agreeing no doubt with the old proverb, which says that in this world " good people are scarce."

He was anxious to return to the " Home," but, fortunately, we did not need his services, for after his departure to the camp a friend had kindly recommended us a young Greek lad as servant. His name was Georgie. He was a great improvement upon Papafée, though not quite so talented as that remarkable individual. This, however, was amply compensated for, by his obedience and extreme anxiety to give us satisfaction. A Greek boy's dress is striking; the full loose trousers, gathered in at the knee, the striped pink cotton shirt, Tartar scarf round the waist, deep blue jacket, crimson fez, white stockings and polished shoes, is altogether very picturesque. Georgie's language was a mixture of Greek, Turkish, Italian, French, and a few words of English. His eagerness to understand what we said was most amusing. If we asked for anything he stood looking at us very earnestly—his black eyes wide open and his finger in his mouth as if they would help him to understand our meaning. Sometimes he would shake his head and say, " No understandie, missie; Georgie no speak much English!" But if happy enough to catch the meaning, his eyes would sparkle and he would dart off like an arrow to execute his commission.

One of our party was anxious to copy some hymn tunes used in the little hospital church. We had no piano, but the wife of one of the civilian doctors kindly offered us the use of hers whenever we had time to walk to her house at Candalee. To accomplish this we had to climb some very steep hills, and as it was not safe to go alone the lady told Georgie to get ready to accompany her.

" Ah, bono mademoiselle," said Georgie, " very good, indeed ! " with a look of intense delight, and off he ran.

In half an hour he returned, dressed in full holiday attire.

" Ah, Georgie, how smart you look ! "

"Ah, mademoiselle, Georgie go with you; very good, much pleasure, so Georgie make himself smart."

She set out, followed by her very amusing page, who united the respectful manners of an English servant with the simplicity and affection of a child.

The road to Candalee is for some distance along a narrow path, on each side of which are houses in a continuous line; it then winds up the hill, which is extremely steep, and without shade; the full glare of the sun, therefore, falls upon one.

At last they reached the summit of the hill and descended into a ravine. Georgie's delight seemed to increase till, as we passed a vineyard full of beautiful grapes, in he rushed and began vigorously gathering the best bunches, asking the lady to take as many as she pleased.

" No, no, Georgie," replied she ; " come away quick—you very naughty—grapes not yours."

" Yes, yes, signora," cried he, " me quite good ; they my bruder's grapes ; he live other side hill up there ; you come see him by and bye ; he like you take plenty—no pay, all complimento." He gathered bunch after bunch.

She thought it very odd, but having become accustomed to odd things in Turkey ceased to remonstrate, only begging him to make haste. He led her through the vineyard and up the next hill where, sure enough, was a little cottage, or rather shed, where he said his " bruder " lived, who it appears kept a vineyard and sold grapes at Constantinople or in the neighbourhood. Georgie made her sit down, and then fetched his bruder and seester—she appearing to be about sixty, and he, seventy years of age. Georgie was about eighteen.

"These are your father and mother, are they not?" said the lady.

"Oh no, my pater is morto," said Georgie, pointing to the ground. "These my bruder and seester, signora."

We suppose they were in reality his aunt and uncle; they were most polite and kind, offering figs, melons, and grapes, and urging their visitor to partake of some, and take the rest home with her.

The whole scene was most picturesque—the young Greek boy in his holiday dress, and the old man and woman with their Eastern hospitality. After resting awhile, with many thanks the lady went her way, and, after copying the music, returned home—Georgie having employed the time during which he was waiting for her in making bouquets for her and the other ladies at the Home. One great pleasure of these Greek boys was to present us with flowers; they were very grateful and affectionate, and so pleased with any little present we gave them, which they always called " complimento."

One day Miss —— gave Georgie a small print of the Crucifixion; he walked about the garden kissing it and pressing it to his heart. On another occasion he was ill in bed with a very bad foot; he slept in a small shed adjoining the Home. Miss —— took him some copies of the *Illustrated News* to amuse him, only intending to lend them, Georgie then expressed his thanks by kissing her hand, evidently taking it for a " complimento;" and behold the next day the walls of his room were adorned with the sheets of the *Illustrated News* pasted all over them!

Ramazan commenced in June; it lasts thirty days. The Turks fast till sunset, both from eating, drinking, and smoking; the two latter privations make it very hard work, as ordinarily a Turk never has his pipe from his lips, and the heat causes great thirst. Shortly before sunset the Turkish troops assemble in the barrack-yard with their large copper dishes; rice is portioned out to them, sometimes mixed with a sort of gravy, and they stand still looking at it till the welcome sound of the sunset gun (which is fired the moment the sun sinks below the horizon) is heard, and then they set to with good appetites to enjoy their dirty-looking dinner.

The caidjees greatly object to taking passengers when near sunset time, but if persuaded to do so and the gun is heard they will stop at the nearest village to get their pipes lighted before they will proceed.

After sunset throughout Ramazan all peace and quiet is over. After the Turks have done eating they begin shouting and dancing and what they call music, a sound resembling that which would be produced in England by one hundred hurdy-gurdies, all playing together. The noise is distracting, and generally lasts until two or three in the morning. It was annoying even to those in the Home, but the officers, whose quarters were close beside the Turkish barracks, complained bitterly of the impossibility of sleeping in consequence of it. All were thankful when the fast drew to its close.

Some of the English residents advised us strongly not to lose the sight of Bairam or Beiram, the Great Feast which follows Ramazan. This was a matter of difficulty, living the distance we did from Constantinople, but through the kindness of friends some of our party were able to have the enjoyment.

The ceremonies of Beiram are as follows : The Sultan must be in Santa Sophia at sunrise, after which he receives in the gardens of his Seraglio his Ministers of State and the chief men of the empire. There are two feasts called by this name commanded to be observed by Mahomet—the first, or the Greater Bairam, is kept at Mecca only when victims are sacrificed, and it is called by the Arabs " Id al Korbam, il al adha," *i. e.*, "The Feast of the Sacrifice," which is celebrated in memory of the sacrifice of Abraham.

But the feast we were about to witness is called the Lesser Bairam, or in Arabia, " Id al Feti." It is dependent on the new moon ; if the sky is so cloudy that she cannot be discerned, the feast is postponed for one day, but after that it proceeds whether they see her or not. Watchers are placed on the surrounding hills to catch the first glimpse of her appearance, and then they run to the city, crying, " Welcome news," and the festivity commences.

We were obliged to quit Koulali at two A.M., to reach Stamboul in time. Çaiques were engaged, and the Turkish sergeant-major volunteered to go as interpreter. This worthy was a remarkable character in the

hospital. He prided himself on his knowledge of English, small though it certainly
was. He took the opportunity of our row
down the Bosphorus to inquire into the
manners and customs of England—to ask
about the pay of English sergeant-majors—
to inform us that his own was sixpence
a-day—to say that he admired the English
more than the Turks, and intended to visit
that country and enter its service, and indeed
his anxiety to visit England was so great
that he offered himself to us in the capacity
of *cook*, if we would only take him. The
grimaces he made, and his gesticulations with
his broken English, and his excessive amusement at our few Turkish words was like
this, "English very bono; Turk no bono;
English soldier how much? Turk soldier so
much; I go you? hidi England; I you
cook; ship hidi Angleterre; very bono,"
and so on.

The night was very dark, but as our

caiques glided down the Bosphorus the
banks were continually illuminated by the
flashes of firearms which were incessantly
fired from the batteries on the hills and
from the Sultan's numerous palaces.   So
continual was this discharge that the Bosphorus was a blaze of light.   As one flash
died away another sprang up, and the hills
gave back the echo of the cannon's thunder.

As we approached Stamboul the morning
had begun to dawn.   The first rays of the
sun gilded the imperial city.   We were not
there yet.   We had to pass through the
Golden Horn and disembark near Seraglio
Point.   It was my first visit to Stamboul
or Istamboul, as it is rightly called, and
what a flood of memories of the "old his-
toric page" came over me as I felt I was
about to enter this ancient and far-famed
city!   How the long train of her eventful
history rose before my mind!   First one's
thoughts wandered back to old Byzantium

and her mighty fortifications, when her
walls were as though of one single block,
1263 years before Christ, so lost in the mist
of ages we can hardly trace it; but we know
well those old walls withstood many a shock.
Siege and assault were matters full of interest to us, and we remembered the walls
and the towers, and the showers of stones
which greeted the besiegers, and, lastly, the
cables of the ships woven of the women's
hair.   Alas! we doubt whether the patriot-
ism of modern ladies would carry them thus
far.

Years pass on and Byzantium becomes a
Christian city.   Constantine the Great sits
on the imperial throne; the idol temples
are thrown down; the old walls ring with
Christian worship.   The Cross by which
Constantine conquered stands in the public
places.   Byzantium was a name that passed
away, and the conqueror named the city
after his own name Constantinople, and he

forsakes even Rome for his new possession.
Constantine averred it was by the especial
command of Heaven that he traced out the
walls of the new city. Nocturnal visions
had guided him. On foot, lance in hand,
and followed by a long procession, the Emperor marked out the boundaries, and the
astonished people at length observed that he
had already exceeded the most ample measure of a great city.

"I shall still advance," said Constantine,
"till He the invisible Guide who marches
before me thinks proper to stop."

Years passed on. The long line of Con-
stantines fill the throne. What scenes of
strife and bloodshed went on within those
old walls! Five hundred years after Constantine had died, the storm of the great
schism is heard. Then the Ottoman power
advances, attacks, makes visible inroads into
the great empire, till at last, in 1453, the
Mussulman reigns in that proud city.

And now our caique touches the quay, and
we come back to the realities of Turkish life
in 1855, not so much unlike 1453 as might
be supposed.   We left our caiques and
walked about a mile to the open plain before
the Seraglio, where the Sultan was staying,
and from whence he would pass to Santa
Sophia.   Stamboul was all alive.   Pashas
with their trains were busily riding hither
and thither.   A large body of Turkish troops
were drawn up in the square awaiting his
Majesty.   Visitors of all nations swelled the
throng.

We waited here about an hour, amusing
ourselves by walking up and down and watching the evolutions of the Pashas on horseback.   The enormous size of some of the
Pashas made the management of their steeds
a matter of difficulty.   They certainly gave
one the impression of a considerable falling
off from the courage of their great ancestors,
whose valour was such that neither Cyrus

nor Alexander could conquer them. Judging
by the streets, manufactories, and public
buildings of the city the genius of their great
father Turk, the son of Japhet, from whom
they so proudly trace their origin, has van-
ished too.

Now the procession began to form. First
came three or four carriages, containing the
Sultanas and other ladies very gaily attired.
Now the Sultan's horses were led out, their
trappings of embroidered silk and jewels;
then came many a Pasha with his train. At
length the "Commander of the Faithful,"
surrounded by his guards, and on horseback.
He was dressed in uniform, over which was
thrown a cloak of dark blue cloth, fastened
by a buckle of brilliants; he wore the crimson fez, in which was a plume of heron's
feathers, secured by a diamond clasp. The
simplicity of his dress formed a striking contrast to his magnificently attired Pashas'.

Slowly the procession passed to Santa So-

phia—the Turkish troops cheering the
Sultan as he proceeded along the line in deep
solemn tones, very unlike the hearty, joyous
cheering of our own land. A dense mass of
people followed. We reached the entrance
of the mosque, and beheld the floor entirely
covered with Turks all prostrate with their
foreheads on the ground. The Imauns at
the door furiously refused admittance to
Franks. One naval officer had contrived to
slip in, and, in answer to all their violent
gesticulations, held up his shoes with an
earnest look to let them see how *much* he had
sacrificed to their prejudices, and he kept his
place, for they dared not lay violent hands
on an officer in uniform.

No wonder they did not want any Franks
if they really followed the universal custom
at Beiram, and prayed either for the rooting
out of all Christian princes, or that they might
quarrel among themselves. It would be
curious if they prayed in 1855 for the over-

throw of Queen Victoria, Louis Napoleon, and Victor Emanuel; perhaps they thought, provided Alexander went too, it did not much signify if the Allies accompanied him.

Owing to our being accompanied by an officer we gained admittance to the Seraglio gardens, and saw the Sultan pass through them on his return to the palace. We waited there about an hour while he took some refreshment. A throne was now placed immediately before the palace covered with crimson velvet; a carpet of the same material at its foot. An open space was cleared, around which were ranged troops. Opposite the throne was the royal band, and we and other strangers ranged ourselves behind the soldiers.

It was a beautiful " presence chamber"— those lovely gardens, and beneath the shade of the old green trees—the cloudless summer sky for his canopy, to receive his Court in. Several ladies and numbers of French

and English officers stood around. Conspi-
cuous amongst them was Monsieur Soyer,
whose costume always marked him out.

At last the Sultan appeared; he walked
up ungracefully to his throne and seated
himself. We were in a position to get an
excellent view of him and of the whole pro-
ceedings. He is a thin, pale, dark, wearied-
looking man, giving one the impression of a
person void of energy, and who would fain
be rid of a heavy burden.

As soon as he was seated, the Pashas
began to walk before him in procession—
some kissing their sovereign's hand, others
only bowing low to the ground before him;
then the Beys followed in order. The
Pashas and Beys were all in European
dress, with the exception of the crimson fez;
but their dresses were covered with rich embroidery. Then came the Imauns, hundreds
of them, of different degrees and rank. All
bowed low before him, making the salaam, *i.e.*,

putting their right hand first to their fore-
head, then to their breast, and bending their
heads nearly to the ground. Some of these,
apparently of higher rank or dignity, kissed
the Sultan's feet, or rather the hem of his
robe; others merely kissed the fringe of
a long scarf which was passed over his
shoulders, and held by one of his chief
officers at some little distance from the
royal person.

Whenever the Imauns, dressed in the
sacred green (the descendants of Mahomet)
approached, the Sultan rose and extended his
hand for them to kiss, which they did with
the utmost reverence. He continued standing quite erect till they passed out of his
sight. The whole scene was most striking,
nearly all the Imauns being dressed in
different colours—white, red, yellow, or
green, in all their shades—and the last in
blue, the only one wearing that colour.
All wore a high white turban, except the

descendants of the Prophet, who were dressed entirely in green, turban and all.

During the pauses in the procession, which sometimes occurred, the Turkish band played; and, although the music was very inferior to that heard in our own land, yet it sounded rather sweetly that early morning in the beautiful Seraglio gardens and added greatly to the romance of the whole scene. When they had all passed, which was not till about eight o'clock A.M., the Sultan rose and departed as ungracefully as he had entered, not even bowing to those around. The festivity of Beiram lasts three days, and incessant firing of cannon goes on day and night.

The assembly broke up, and we were not sorry; for the fatigue of six hours' standing, after a sleepless night, was very great. When we reached our caiques, the sun had become glaringly hot, and making our voyage home a most disagreeable one; so that we could hardly listen to the incessant conversation of the Sergeant-Major, who now quite changed his tone, and did nothing but extol the greatness of Turkey, its Sultan, and Pashas.

CHAPTER VII.

Sultry weather—Cholera cases—The nuns' careful
nursing—A cargo of ice—A fortunate speculatio
—Remarkable cases of cholera in the Barrack Hospital—Smoking allowed—Mosquitoes—A voyage in
the ice-ship—An unsuccessful attempt to visit the
Black Sea—The sick doctor—Admitted into the hospital at Koulali—Carefully nursed there—An awful
spectacle—The closing scene—Health of the nursing
staff—Kindness of the Army surgeons.

THE heat at the end of July grew intense,
and continued so till the end of the following
month. Up to this time it had been like a very
warm English summer; but now the Eastern
sun poured down all its fury upon us, and
we were terribly exposed to its rays. No
kind of shade was at hand: there was hardly
a tree in Koulali. The five minutes' walk

from our home to hospital, was along the quay.

The Sisters of Mercy, who came down from the General Hospital and returned thither twice a-day, had to descend and climb the steep hill in the glaring sun; so, also, the ladies who worked at the General Hospital. Our hospital duties obliged us to be walking about during the greater part of the time when the inhabitants of the country close their jalousies and take their siesta, not venturing to move till sunset.

The heat was real suffering; it brought incessant thirst, which nothing could quench. The quantity of lemonade which was drank during that time was something marvellous, and it seemed impossible to touch the meat of the country; and yet too great a quantity of acid, and the omission of strengthening food, was considered very dangerous, as likely to bring on cholera.

We feared that cholera would have been

very prevalent in the summer—thank God
it was not so!—twenty was the utmost of
those attacked, and out of these not more
than half were fatal. At the General Hospital were several bad cases, whose lives
were saved, humanly speaking, by the
attention they received from the nuns, who
watched by them day and night.

A great blessing arrived about this period,
in the shape of ice; it was sent out by
government. The ship that brought it was
called the "City of Montreal," her captain
was a Scotchman; he purchased a cargo of ice
in North America at a venture, which proved
a fortunate one, for three days after coming
into Liverpool the whole was bought by
government, and he was instantly despatched
with it to the East. Part was left at Scutari,
part at Koulali, the rest went to Balaclava.
The captain reckoned he had made £500 by
the enterprise. Thankful indeed were we
that he had made it.

There was an ice-house at the General Hospital into which the ice was put, and we used to send the Greeks to fetch it down to the Barrack. Unfortunately the ice-house was not a good one, and the ice melted faster than it would otherwise have done; so we were obliged to use it as fast as possible, but it lasted the exact time the extreme heat did. I cannot think what we should have done without it. Certainly we could not have given " cooling drinks " any longer, for the lemonade used to be quite warm till iced ; and it was such a comfort to the fever patients to lay on their burning brows, and most useful in cholera ; also in obstinate cases of diarrhœa and dysentery it checked vomiting and allayed the irritation of the stomach.

There were two cases of cholera in the Barrack Hospital which were remarkable ; they were in different wards, one in the surgical the other in the dysentery ; their symptoms were exactly similar, consisting chiefly in extreme depression; they resisted all nourishment and wept almost incessantly, and no one could discover that they had any particular cause for grief. Both these cases were fatal.

Smoking was ordered in the wards when cholera was about; this was rather amusing to the men as they had been before strictly forbidden to smoke in the wards, and it had been a great deprivation to those not able to walk into the barrack-yard, for unless a man were in a dying state he had strength enough for his beloved pipe; even while it was forbidden they would smoke whenever they could do so without being seen.

Another misery brought by the heat was the increase of vermin. Mosquitos began to pay us a visit; they never abounded so much as we expected, but they were quite bad enough, and their bite was very painful and disfiguring. We had mosquito-net from the stores, which we cut into squares and threw it over the faces of those who were very ill. Fleas abounded and were very tormenting; we used a powder which can be bought at Stampa's shop in Galata, and to all Eastern travellers I should recommend it; for though it does not destroy these enemies, it stupifies them, and one has the satisfaction of seeing the sheets spread with them fast asleep, while otherwise the wretches are so very rapid in their movements that it is almost a hopeless undertaking to wage war against them. From their facility in making their escape, some one named them the "light cavalry," while *other horrors* which we occasionally had the misfortune to encounter in the wards, who were not so light of foot, were called " heavy dragoons."

The ice ship lay off Koulali for several days. The captain used to send his boat in the evening to know if we would like to have

a row, and as it held a great many we were
glad to take the nurses out in it.   When the
" City of Montreal " was ready to proceed to
Balaclava it was proposed that two or three
ladies should go on board of her as far as the
entrance to the Black Sea, and return in the
steamer which would tug her up to that
point.   She was to start at six A.M.

We went on board one lovely morning ;
the steamer began to tug the vessel, but
could not succeed.   The current was so
strong that she was powerless, and after
trying for two hours in vain she was obliged
to give it up.   The steamers used for tug-
ging are the small ones which ply upon the
Bosphorus and are hired by the Admiralty.
The " City of Montreal " was tugged up
next day by the " Ottawar," a fine steam-
ship.

We did not attempt to see the Black Sea
a second time, having been so disappointed
the first day, so we contented ourselves

with having seen the Euxine from Therapia without actually passing into its waters.

One day a ship came alongside Koulali wharf to coal; she had on board a Dr. Thompson and his wife. Dr. Thompson was a civilian, who had practised for some years in Antioch, before that I think in India, and was well known for scientific discoveries.

It appeared that he had wished to visit Balaclava, and had proceeded thither, accompanied by his wife; while there—living on board ship—was seized with the Crimean fever. When the ship was obliged to return he was too ill to be moved, and indeed at Balaclava there was no place for him. The vessel came to Scutari, and application was made to the authorities for his admission into the hospital.

An unfortunate delay arose about granting this, which no doubt would have been done at length. The vessel could not wait; having discharged her cargo for Scutari she came to Koulali, Dr. Thompson still on board. The same application was made at Koulali, and was instantly granted; Koulali being a much smaller place than Scutari it had probably not to go through so many hands before it was decided on. At all events they were received.

The heat was so intense that though it was granted at noon they were forced to wait till the cool evening before they dared move him—for he was raving in delirium, and his fever was in the highest stage. Meanwhile, an empty ward in the General Hospital was prepared for his use, and everything which the hospital possessed in the way of comfort placed at his disposal by Dr. Humphrey, P. M. O. Our Superintendent appointed one of her best nurses to aid Mrs. Thompson in attending on him, and committed him also to the care of the reverend Mother.

From that day for weeks the one topic of the hospital was Dr. Thompson. If he had been a king more could not have been done for him; his delirium was very violent, and he would take dislikes to the surgeons and want new ones. Accordingly, almost every one in the hospital went to him at any time he chose to ask for them. He appeared to be fond of music, and it was thought singing would soothe him. One of the ladies accordingly went and sang to him for hours.

The Sisters of Mercy were most unremitting in their attentions, especially the reverend Mother, who was called up night after night, and who cheerfully hastened to see if she could in any way relieve him. Fatigue and distress had their effect upon poor Mrs. Thompson, her grief was violent, and she required much attention. The reverend Mother spent much time in soothing her, sometimes reading a few verses of the

Holy Scriptures or a hymn. Mrs. Thompson spoke of her kindness afterwards with much gratitude.

Dr. Thompson and his wife were members of the Church of England. The chaplain visited them constantly, and he also used to be called up in the night when the delirium was at its height that he might endeavour to quiet the sufferer.

There was at one time a slight hope of his recovery, but an abscess, which was a frequent result of the Crimean fever, gathered in his neck, and death fast approached. The nurse who had been waiting on him, being worn out, returned to rest. Another whom we thought well of took her place, and a few hours after worse symptoms appeared.

Word of this being brought to the lady superintendent, she went at 11 p.m. to the General Hospital to see him. Upon entering the room the scene was awful. He was in his last agony, his wife was by his side doing all she believed best for him. On a bed that had been standing in the room lay the nurse in a state of dead intoxication. She had, while passing from the Home to the hospital (the emergency having obliged her to be sent alone), purchased the Turkish spirits, which produce a perfect stupor. She could not be awakened, and the superintendent was obliged to call four orderlies to carry her upstairs, where she lay for hours in the same state.

All through the night the superintendent watched beside the sick bed. The chaplain came and read the commendatory prayers, and finding reason was not likely to return then left him. At Mrs. Thompson's desire the Presbyterian chaplain afterwards came and prayed beside him, and about 3 p.m. he expired.

His body was interred the following day in Koulali British burying-ground; all the medical staff followed in uniform.

Many of the ladies and nurses also attended to accompany his widow, whose wish
it was to be present.

During life Dr. Thompson had often expressed a wish to be buried beneath a tree,
and in sight of a beautiful view.   There was
but one tree in the burying-ground; under
that they dug his grave, while all around lay
spread one of the most beautiful scenes one
could imagine.

During the whole summer only one case
of serious illness occurred amongst our
party.   Miss F—— lay for many weeks ill
with dysentery.   She was attended by Dr.
Guy, and to his extreme attention and skill,
under God's blessing, she owed her recovery.
After a time she resumed her work.   There
was a great deal of sickness amongst us,
though not of a serious character, but almost
all suffered from the heat extremely.

In our illnesses we were attended only
by the army surgeons, and they were kind

beyond measure.   About this time, to our
great regret, Dr. Temple joined the Turkish
Contingent; there was great mourning among
his patients at his departure, for he was one
of the kindest as well as the most skilful of
the surgeons.

CHAPTER VIII.

Miss Stanley's interview with Her Majesty, Queen Vic-
toria—The Royal gifts—The Queen's letter—The
Illustrated London News—Division of the Royal gifts
—Chess, dominoes, and draughts—Frequent fires in
Constantinople—An alarm of fire—Fears dispelled—
The palace of the Sultan's sister—Swift destruction
—A magnificent spectacle — Establishment of an
hospital library—Variety of the book gifts—Bibles
and Prayer-books.

ONE day we received a letter from Miss
Stanley, with an account of an interview she
had had with the Queen, who sent for her
and inquired with the deepest interest into
the details of our work, and wished to know
what more she could send out to contribute
to the comfort of the sick and to assure them
of her continual sympathy. The interview
lasted near an hour, and at its close her Ma-

jesty expressed her satisfaction at what she had heard, and her thanks for the service rendered. Miss Stanley also received the thanks of Prince Albert and the Duchess of Kent on a subsequent occasion.

She transmitted the royal thanks to us, feeling, as she said, she had only received them as the representative of all who had done the work.

In the royal gifts which came out a short time afterwards, we recognised the articles which Miss Stanley had named in answer to her Majesty's inquiries. The pleasure these gifts of her Majesty gave was immense; they consisted of a large quantity of raspberry jam, treacle, tamarinds, and pickles. Also chess, dominoes, and draughts.

The gifts were valuable in themselves, but how much more so the remembrance of the thoughtful sympathy that had sent them out.

"Only to think of our Queen thinking of

such things for the like of us," said the patients.

But they had already grown familiar with the knowledge that the sufferings of the soldiers in camp and hospital were no less remembered in the palace than in their humble homes.

In all the wards was posted upon the walls the beautiful letter written by Queen Victoria to Mr. Sidney Herbert in the month of December 1854, and which caused such a thrill of gratitude and delight among the soldiers.

The *Illustrated London News*, which were distributed among them, had shown them how their Queen " visited the sick." They saw her passing through hospital wards and speaking gentle words to the sufferers there. They heard of her warm interest in all they did or suffered, and that no hand but her own was allowed to decorate their comrades who had returned home.

The royal gifts were divided by the purveyor-in-chief, among the different Eastern
hospitals. Pickles were only allowed by the
medical officers for the convalescent patients,
for whom doubtless her Majesty intended
them. Jam and treacle were used in all
the wards; the latter many men preferred to
butter; but the portion of the royal gifts
which gave most delight were the chess, dominoes, and draughts.

The authorities of course informed her
Majesty of the gratitude and delight with
which her bounty had been received; but
those official letters told her but a small part.
We often wished the Queen could have *once*
seen what we saw daily; the groups of men
gathered round the table at those games, the
extreme pleasure they gave them, the time
they innocently employed, and the temptations of drink and idle company from which
they kept them.

For ourselves, these royal gifts were not

without a peculiar pleasure, as it showed us
plainly that her Majesty did not esteem common necessaries enough for her gallant army,
but was determined that comforts, and even a
few luxuries, should be poured upon them,
and that she approved of our efforts to bring
these to the men.   Cheering to us in that far
off land and amidst our many difficulties
was the kind sympathy of our beloved Queen.

Every traveller to Constantinople has
spoken of the frequent fires.   I do not
know whether they were more numerous
than usual this summer ; but certainly
they were almost incessant.   People said
that at times it was done on purpose, the
Sultan wishing to destroy some of the dirty
wooden houses ; but I think this is improb-
able.   They generally occurred at night.
We always knew they were going on by
the firing of seven guns from the Turkish
battery on the hill above Koulali.   Sometimes we rose and looked, for the sight was

very fine ; but at last they grew so frequent that they hardly roused us.

One night a discharge of cannon was heard. I had grown so used to it, that I concluded it was the first of the seven guns, and did not disturb myself. A noise in the house attracted my attention. I rose, and, going into the corridor, found the whole household assembled and gazing out of the corridor windows with looks of alarm. *Apparently* the General Hospital was on fire. Our first thought was for the Sisters of Mercy : the patients, we knew, would be carried to the Barrack Hospital ; but the Sisters would be homeless.

Two of us dressed in haste, and went out. As we approached the foot of the hill, a body of troops rushed down. They perceived us, and a sergeant stopped to inform us that some gunpowder, kept in a shed not far from the General Hospital, had taken fire and exploded, which was the sound we heard.

No danger had occurred, and no lives were
lost, though, on the first alarm, all the troops,
British and Turkish, were turned out; and
the sergeant declared he was asleep, dream-
ing Sebastopol was taken, and when the
sudden call came, he thought it was to
summon him to the assault.

We hastened home to quell the anxiety
of our companions; and the alarm over, the
laughing began, as we who had been out declared they all looked like Turkish ladies in
feridgees, sitting on the divan of the corridor.

When the day came, we went to congratu-
late the Sisters on their escape. They said
they had been much alarmed, the explosion
being so very near their apartments; and
when they were awakened by the sudden
noise, and immediately afterwards the tramp
of the troops coming up the hill, one of
them confessed she thought the Russians had
come! at which we all laughed very much.

One morning when we came down to

prayers we saw a fire on the opposite coast.
The villages are so thickly joined together
that we could hardly distinguish where it
was. It was a palace of the Sultan, said to
belong to the Sultan's sister. If it was this
palace, one was not sorry to see it burnt
down; for horrible traditions attach to the
name of Asma, Sultan Mahmoud's sister;
and, it is said, from underneath a low arch
bodies were often seen to float into the
Bosphorus from her palace.

Whether it was her palace or not, it was
in flames, and in half-an-hour was destroyed,
for it was of course built of wood, and a
strong breeze blew from the Black Sea, and
the work of devastation was rapid.

Many houses stood near whose owners
were in great alarm. Next to them came
a grove of cypresses, and a large villa beyond them stood higher up the hill. Curi-
ously enough the flames did not touch
the adjoining houses. We thought when

we saw the palace falling into pieces that its
fury was spent, when suddenly behind the·
cypresses the forked flames burst out, catching the villa and destroying it. It is thus
that the fires in Turkey spread, so that
when they once begin the whole village
often falls. In this case, however, when
the villa was burnt the fire was arrested.

It was a striking sight to see the volume
of bright flame behind those dark trees,
which it did not attempt to touch, and lower
down the hill the burning blackened ruins of
the palace, falling piece by piece into the blue
Bosphorus, while the lurid glare of the fire
mingled with the bright sunshine of that
cloudless summer morning.

During the summer the hospital library
was established. A large room fitted with
shelves was given for this purpose. It was
under the charge of Mr. Coney, the Church
of England chaplain. He requested the ladies
would assist him in getting it into order.

The superintendent had no one whom she could send, so she added the charge to her own numerous duties. The task of sorting and arranging was a long and tedious one. Numbers of cases arrived and contained many nice books; but a quantity of rubbish among them, reports of charities, old ency-clopædias, &c., &c. Then would come most provoking *portions* of books; fragments of all the Waverley novels, with not one complete; odd numbers of ancient magazines. Next would come a number of little books for Sunday scholars, which we certainly deemed as much below the capacity of the men as the number of essays on abstruse subjects which were sent were above them. A great many nice books came too. Mr. Albert Smith's handsome present had arrived long months before; but of course many of his books furnished the library shelves.

The arrangement of the library was a

great comfort. Before it was opened the
books were kept in the chaplain's quarters;
we used to go there and hunt through the
cases for the kind we wanted. Now they
were all arranged in order. Bibles and
prayer-books by themselves, religious books
in another part, instructive works in a third,
and the novels and tales in a fourth; magazines by themselves, while those who wished
to read the mutilated Waverley, &c. could
find them on a top shelf.

There was a good store of Bibles and
prayer-books, but we were always asking
for more from England, as the chaplains
gave them to each man not possessing them
when he left either for home or camp.

The Catholic religious books were generally sent to the Catholic chaplain or Sisters.
If they came into the library they were forwarded to them. Five hundred Catholic
Testaments were sent by kind friends, and
were much valued. Other packets of books

arrived, but many others shared the frequent fate of parcels to the East, and never reached their destination.

Several hundreds of Scotch Bibles with the Psalms, as used in the Kirk, came to the general library, and were forwarded by Mr. Coney to the Presbyterian chaplain for the exclusive use of his congregation.

Secular books were of course for all classes alike, and, after they had been sorted, the ladies and sisters had free access to the library, and could take as many as they pleased. How the men did delight in those books ! Every ward had a little lending library of its own, books taken from the general library, and lent and changed from one to another all round the ward. Books were sent out by the Duchess of Kent; amongst them were many copies of St. John's history of the present war which was a great favourite.

CHAPTER IX.

Chaplains appointed to Koulali—Arrangements respecting the various services—The ward used for the English service—Establishment of daily morning prayers—The Sunday congregation—Singing classes in Koulali hospital—The Presbyterian services—The Catholic priest—Beneficial results of his exertions—Morning sunlight on Constantinople—The religious spirit in the British army—Its previous neglect—The honourable cowardice of a brave man.

THERE were three chaplains appointed to Koulali—the Church of England, the Catholic, and the Presbyterian (sometimes there were two of the first-mentioned). When the wards were so crowded no place was set apart for public worship, and the men being chiefly in their beds or unable to walk, it was only the men on duty who attended the services. At that time the English and Scotch services were held at respective hours on Sundays only, in the detachment ward in the morning or the convalescent hospital in the afternoon.

The Catholic services were daily in the Sisters' oratory in the General Hospital, where the men could attend, and on Sundays in the chaplain's own room in the Barrack Hospital; when the summer came on and it became evident that the new wards which had been fitted up in the winter would never all be filled, one was given to the English chaplain, a room in the General Hospital to the Catholic, and another empty ward in the Barrack to the Presbyterian.

The ward used for the English service was the one fronting the Sultan's apartments. The roof was sloping and not very high; it was very wide and would have made a fine ward. It was four times too large for its purpose, as the congregation only filled half one side.

Up to the time of Mr. Coney's arrival the services were only on Sundays (except Ash Wednesday and Good Friday). Soon after he became senior chaplain he established daily morning prayers ; and the communion, which had been administered monthly, was now given every Sunday at 7.30 A.M.

The purveyor-in-chief had the ward furnished with church fittings, and some of the ladies aided to beautify it, and it looked very nice when finished, though of course rudely adorned. The altar rails were of plain deal, a red cloth covered the table, and the reading-desk was hung with the same colour. A few benches were arranged on each side, some with backs to them were also placed lower down for the invalids, and the wooden trestles of the empty beds formed seats for the rest of the congregation.

This congregation on Sunday made a singular scene. The different groups : a number of men on duty in their uniforms,

then a mass of blue dressing-gowns and
white night-caps, another of nurses in grey
dresses, the ladies seated among them either
in black or colours; on the other side the
officers also in uniform, one or two officers'
wives, and sometimes a few English strangers from the neighbouring village of Bebek,
on the European side, the only Protestant
service there being in the Protestant Armenian chapel, and the singing was so
atrocious, they said, they preferred coming
across to Koulali, where the singing was
very good considering its difficulties. There
being no instrument it was led by one of the
ladies who had a singing-class twice a-week,
which the convalescent patients and some of
the sergeants and detachment men attended.
They were very fond of coming to it, and
took great pains to learn the chants and
hymn tunes; those they had been accustomed
to hear in the churches at home pleased
them most.

The Presbyterian service was at the same hour as the English one. The members of this congregation were fewer than either the English or Catholic churches. Two of the ladies of our party and one of the nurses belonged to it. Many of the Presbyterian soldiers appeared to be earnest and religious men. The chaplain was exceedingly active in visiting the sick members of his congregation.

The Catholic chapel was arranged with great taste, though of course with the greatest simplicity; the altar was raised on the divan, which fronted the windows. The room was furnished with benches, the middle space left for the men and officers, the sisters kneeling on each side. A few coloured prints hung on the wall; everything was very rough, but all the essentials of Catholic worship were there. The services were well attended by the men. The two masses on Sundays (one at each hospital) were crowded;

the daily mass had a good gathering, and so had the Sunday benediction.

The chaplain for many months was Mr. Ronan ; this priest was most zealous and devoted, beloved by his flock, and respected by all. The improvement among the Catholics in Koulali was very great. The soldiers had been much neglected, and many had yielded to temptation, contracted evil habits, and forgotten their religion, but the efforts made by the priests and nuns were blessed. Those who had lived long years in sin once more sought their Saviour—those whose last remembrance of prayers and sacraments had been in days gone by, in the shelter of their homes, now returned to the God of their youth.

Were these pages the fitting place many a tale might be told of such, but they are not. It will, however, interest Catholics to hear that the Sisters of Mercy had the satisfaction of knowing that no member of their church ever left the hospitals of Koulali without receiving the sacraments, nor did any die without their consolations.

It will interest others to know among the members of the Church of England a marked improvement took place — many turning from evil or careless lives and becoming earnest and zealous in religion, thus rewarding their good chaplain's labours, who spared no pains in the performance of his duty. When Mr. Coney established the daily morning prayers he expected them to be attended by about a dozen at the utmost. To his surprise and pleasure he found more than that come even the first morning, and in a week's time it had increased to thirty or more. The time for prayers was half-past seven in the morning.

Beautiful indeed were those early mornings, before the glaring sun attained its power ; the golden light adorning the distant white walls and towers of Constantinople with a crown of glory. It looked like a visionary city, making one think of THE one for which "we seek," and which "is to come." The dewdrops sparkled on the grass, the clear sweet singing of the birds came through the open windows. The blue ripples of the Bosphorus shone brightly, and our first waking sensations were those of admiration of all this wonderful beauty. When we went out the air was so light and fresh and invigorating.

A little before seven in the morning a group of convalescents, dressed in blue, and soldiers in uniform, were seen climbing the hill to attend mass. Many who were very weak persisted in going, and counted the fatigue nothing in comparison of the blessing they would receive. At half-past seven another group wended their way to the English prayers.

When the heat was gone, and the work had very much diminished, the daily service was altered to nine in the morning, and

when Dr. Freeth succeeded Mr. Coney as
chaplain he established an evening one
at six o'clock. These services were well
attended both by officers and men, who
chanted and sang very heartily at each of
them. The officers seemed to prefer the
later hour in the morning, as now the brunt
of the work was over they were not obliged
to be in their wards so early as in the summer ; this was also the case with some of the
ladies and nurses.

These are plain proofs that the spirit of
real religion is in the British army, and only
needs culture to bring it out, and had not
its spiritual wants been so grievously neglected it would not have become noted for its
irreligion, nor would English parents have
had cause hitherto to consider it a disgrace
that their sons should fill its ranks. The
following anecdotes will show how ready
they were to amend. One orderly bore
a very high character, and was much liked

by the sister of the ward for his good conduct. One day he became intoxicated; when he came to his senses he hid himself from the sister. However, she met him accidentally and expressed her sorrow and displeasure; he had been a soldier for seventeen years, yet he blushed before her as a guilty schoolboy, and exclaimed—

"Oh, ma'am, look it over this time, it never shall happen again; I'd rather be summoned before all the doctors in the hospital and be punished by them, than that you should once reprove me."

Indeed the orderlies at the Upper Hospital thought the sisters' displeasure far worse than being sent to the guardroom.

One day an orderly, partly drunk when the reverend Mother entered the ward, attempted to conceal his state; she turned away and called another, bidding the first go to bed at once. The next day he was ready as usual to carry round the extras for her. "No," she said, "you have disgraced yourself, I will have another." He slunk away ashamed. Some days passed, and she took no notice of him. At last one day he waylaid her in the corridor, where no one could hear him, and said with tears in his eyes, "Will you never forgive me, reverend Mother? I am so miserable to be in disgrace with you—indeed I will amend for the future."

CHAPTER X.

Decrease of the numbers in the hospital—Destination
of those wounded in the attack of the 18th of June—
Regimental and camp hospitals—The Superintendent's
offer to go to the Crimea—Negatived by Lady Stratford
—Application by the Reverend Mother to Dr. Hall—
Departure of the Turkish troops stationed in the
hospital—Hospital wanted for the Sardinians—The
fall of Sebastopol—A soldier's letter relating the
event—Rejoicings and illuminations—One sigh for
the mourners in the hour of victory—The anniversary
of the Alma—Dinner parties on the occasion—An
incident.

SINCE June the numbers in the hospital
had been gradually decreasing, and the character of the cases had completely changed.
Of course, there were exceptions; but as a
rule those who came down from the front
were nearly convalescent, needing only

nourishment or change of air, and accordingly after they had been a few weeks in Koulali they were either invalided home or discharged to duty. When the attack of the 18th of June took place we looked for wounded and sick to come down, but not one arrived, and we then found that the medical and other authorities at head-quarters had determined to keep the sick as much as possible in the Crimea, considering the air there best for them, and the voyage down unadvisable.

The number of regimental hospitals had so increased that they were able to accommodate a large number. There was an hospital in the camp besides the General and Castle Hospitals, Balaclava, for the more serious cases. Besides, except from the attack of the 18th of June, the health of the army was far better than had been expected.

From these various causes arose the circumstance that the hospitals on the Bosphorus were more than half empty. Of course this was a matter of great thankfulness, but the question arose whether our nursing staff was not too large for our work. As time went on we became certain of this, and the accounts which the invalids and others brought from the Crimea, convinced us that the brunt of the work was passed from our hospitals and lay in the Crimea.

We knew that there were but few nurses there, and we were anxious that some of us should proceed there if required, a point we resolved to ascertain. Lord William Paulet was commandant at the time, and he had requested Lady Stratford de Redcliffe to exercise his authority over the nursing department. Our superintendent told Lady Stratford she was ready to go to the Crimea, but Lady Stratford negatived it at once, and in a decided manner. As no other lady was equal to the task of directing so untried and laborious an undertaking, the idea was relinquished.

The reverend Mother soon after this
writing to one of the chaplains, a friend of
hers in the camp, told him how little we had
to do in the hospital, and that she and the
Sisters felt an earnest wish to have work
such as they came to do. She read this
letter to our superintendent, who agreed
with its purport. The chaplain wrote in
answer, that if she would again write and
repeat her statements more formally he
would show it to Dr. Hall. The reverend
Mother did so, expressing in it how willing
she would be either to continue under our
present superintendent if it was thought
desirable, or to go alone with her Sisters.

So the matter rested, and we lived on in
the usual state of uncertainty attending
British affairs in the East. None but those
who have experienced it could enter completely into this feeling. We hardly ever
knew what had happened, or what was going
to happen. Rumours of all kinds so con-

tinually buzzed about that, at last, we learned to believe nothing till we saw it in an English newspaper. The fall of Sebastopol we were told every week had taken place. Every imaginable tale was spread about.

The only incident just at this time was one which gave us some pleasure, in the departure of the Turkish troops stationed at the hospital. We were told the room was to be occupied with Sardinian soldiers. A quantity of boats came to fetch the Turks' baggage—there was a fine quantity of rubbish on the quay. The Turkish soldiers were a miserable-looking set, and we were glad to get rid of them; especially as we heard such a high character of the Sardinian soldiers.

Away the Turks went, but days went on and no Sardinians appeared. Then came in another tale. The Sardinians were badly off for room, especially for their sick. Three officers came one day, walked round our hospitals, and said, on seeing the convalescent hospital, "How happy we should be if we could only get this hospital for our poor sick."

Rumour now said that General Storks, who had by this time succeeded Lord William Paulet in command, was obliged to give the Sardinians room, and he was thinking of giving them our General Hospital; at first we did not credit it, but the story strengthened. We knew the only Sardinian hospital on the Bosphorus was one of huts at Yenikoi, and that long ago when Lord William held the command he had offered them the one at Abydos, which they declined, as being at so great a distance from the camp; but thoughts and plans were suddenly interrupted by the real news that Sebastopol had fallen. There was no doubt: cannon and flags and information from the embassy confirmed this tale. Graphic accounts from our soldier-friends at camp soon arrived. We insert a letter from one of the sergeants, who had been Sister Anne's ward-master.

"Camp before Sebastopol, 16th Sept., 1855.

" Sister Anne,—Sebastopol has fallen! The enemy is in full retreat! The town is in flames since the 8th. The 2nd and Light Divisions attacked the Malakoff and took it without losing a man; but in attacking the Redan, the 88th, 55th, and 71st, and other corps of these divisions, suffered severely in trying to take it. Next morning (9th) we were in full possession of this side of the town and part of the north side too. I send you a piece of Russian riband I found in the town (for the French and English were in it plundering by eight o'clock). I have some small oil paintings yet, but the larger articles I gave them to officers of the corps. Such beautiful furniture I never saw before in any town, and it is a little dangerous to enter it as yet, for all the houses are filled with powder. Perhaps we would be ransacking a house and the next one to us would be blown up. Not many

hurt in the town after all.   Hoping the fall
of this terrible fortress will put an end to
the war and enable the soldiers of the army
to go home to see their friends—the wish of
every one of us here, officers, soldiers, and
sailors—and hoping you will excuse this
scribble,

      " I remain your most obedient servant,
                    "J. J., 28th Regt."

The news seemed to cheer our men's
spirits, who had begun to think that in
spite of all they had done and suffered the
great object of it all would never be accomplished, and that Sebastopol never would
be taken.   They illuminated the hospital
as well as they could by sticking innumerable pieces of tallow candles (which they
either bought or asked the ladies to buy for
them) in every pane of every window, and
in all other imaginable places; they made
candlesticks of common soap, a piece of in-
genuity which much amused us.

There were of course grand illuminations all down the Bosphorus, and beautiful fireworks. The ships were all gaily decorated with flags, and the firing of cannon was tremendous.

In the evening the soldiers made a bonfire outside the hospital, into which they threw everything they could lay hands upon, old packing cases, boxes, chests, firewood, planks, and, lastly, a cart belonging to a Greek which happened to be near; they seized upon it, first threw it into the Bosphorus to see if it would swim, and then dragged it out amid shouts of laughter, and threw it on the blazing fire, round which they danced, and sang songs of battle and victory and "God save the Queen." The commandant and all the officers stood above both sanctioning and enjoying the festivities. We also looked on at a little distance, accompanied by the whole staff of nurses, who fully entered into the excitement of the scene.

We could not help thinking, however, as
we stood listening to the sounds of rejoicing
at the glorious victory, of the many aching
hearts the news of it would cause in England. Alas! with what sickening suspense
would many and many a mother, sister,
wife, and friend watch for the coming lists
of killed and wounded, and sadly how to
many of them would the fall of the great
Sebastopol be the death-blow of their earthly
happiness! True, their loved ones had died
a glorious death in the flush of honour and
victory, but death, whether on the battle-
field or in the silent chamber, is still *death*,
and, as we watched the brilliant illuminations that evening on the shores of the
Bosphorus, and listened to the repeated hur-
rahs, we sorrowfully remembered those who
would weep to-morrow in England.

The 20th of September was the anniversary of the Alma. The soldiers were anxious
to keep the day with honour, and there was

a dinner party organised in each hospital : that at the lower consisted of the non-commissioned officers, at the upper the sergeants and orderlies in charge—for this latter plenty of plum-puddings were made in the extra-kitchen, for we liked to do anything to encourage the orderlies.

When they were about to sit down the reverend Mother spoke to them and begged them to observe temperance and not disgrace themselves. They promised faithfully they would, and when she had retired they drank her health, with the toast, " Long may she reign over us," and every man of the party went to bed sober. They were very much pleased with themselves next morning when they found not one was in the guard-room, while at the Barrack Hospitals there were dozens there.

At the Barrack Hospitals we gave our orderlies plum-puddings, but as they were not invited to the non-commissioned officers' dinner they had them for supper, and

enjoyed them very much; but, alas, they
did not keep in such good order as their
comrades on the hill. Some of the ladies
wishing, with perhaps rather more kindness
than wisdom, to treat their orderlies on this
occasion, gave them a little money, charging
them not to drink more than they ought;
they promised to remember this, and many
kept the promise, but there were a few
exceptions.

In No. 3 Upper was an orderly who was
always too much inclined to drink; in all
other respects he was very valuable, being
extremely kind to the patients and attentive
to orders. Sister M—— A—— had charge
of his ward—when she came next morning
to her ward he was missing—she inquired
again and again for W——, wanting him to
fetch the extras and attend to various other
matters, but no one would tell her where
her orderly was; there was evidently some
mystery connected with him, and at last she

very gently but decidedly insisted upon knowing it.

"Where is W——?" said she, "I want him particularly and cannot wait any longer."

"Well, if you please, Sister, he's on the shelf in the linen-press."

She went to the cupboard, and there sure enough he was fast asleep on one of the shelves, where his comrades had laid him, hoping to shield him from punishment. It was so utterly absurd that she had difficulty in looking grave, and thought it best to let the matter pass; but the ladies, on being told of the circumstance, took care not to treat their orderlies in the same way again.

CHAPTER XI.

Expectations of more patients—The General Hospital
given up to the Sardinians—The Sisters of Mercy
sent for to the General Hospital, Balaclava—Catholic
chaplains in the camp—A busy time—Various accounts of Balaclava—Departure of the Sisters for
Balaclava — Farewells — Departure of the senior
Church of England chaplain—Closing of the General
Hospital, Koulali—Universal admiration felt for the
Sisters of Mercy—Proposed diminution of the Nursing
Staff—Dr. Humphrey and the diet roll—Reasona-
bleness of his return to routine—Resignation of five
of the lady-volunteers.

IMMEDIATELY after Sebastopol fell we were
told 500 sick, either Russian or British, most
likely the former, would arrive. This caused
a great commotion—beds were prepared, the
new wards looked to, and it was proposed to

dismantle the church ward to make room—
fortunately it was decided to wait till the
sick came before this was done. Every day
we looked out for them, and yet they came
not; and at last we found it was only a report, and it began to appear very evident that
the hospitals on the Bosphorus would never,
in all human likelihood, be filled again (for
if the fall of Sebastopol did not bring sick
and wounded nothing else would); and the
work in the trenches being now at an end
the coming winter was not likely to produce
the miseries of the last.

Next came the news that General Storks
had decided upon giving up the General
Hospital to the Sardinians. It was a blow
to lose our pretty model hospital just as it was
perfect—kitchen stores and wards, each a
pattern in its way and all working so well.
Still we felt our regret was rather selfish.
There were not fifty patients in this hospital,
and for these there was abundance of room in

the Barrack Hospital, while our gallant allies,
it was said, were in distress.

Next came a letter from Dr. Hall to the
reverend Mother, asking her and her sisters
to come and take the nursing at the General
Hospital, Balaclava, which had been under
Miss Nightingale's superintendence, and had
been attended through the summer by one
lady and three or four nurses belonging to
Miss Nightingale's staff; but Dr. Hall's
letter said that Miss Nightingale had just resigned the charge of General Hospital, Balaclava, into his hands, informing him that
her nurses would be withdrawn by the 1st of
October.   Dr. Hall, therefore, wished the
Sisters to come as soon as possible after that
day.

He wrote at the same time to our principal
medical officer requesting him to make the
necessary arrangements for their departure,
and apply for passages.

The reverend Mother asked our superin-

tendent if she could spare her, and though
Miss Hutton's regret at losing the Sisters was
very great, she said she could not conscien-
tiously hinder them and gave her permission
for their departure, and aided in their preparations.

A Catholic chaplain from the camp, Mr.
Woolett, came down to escort the Sisters to
Balaclava. Mr. Woolett had visited Koulali
several times previously. He had been on
board the same vessel which brought the
ladies and nurses in April, and was therefore
welcomed as a friend; his name was also
familiar to us being so often mentioned by
the patients coming down sick from the
camp who spoke with gratitude of the attention he rendered them. He was indeed one
of the many excellent chaplains who distinguished themselves by their devotion to their
sacred duties in the camp. An interesting history the deeds they have wrought would make
—but most of them are unknown to the world.

In the early spring the number of Catholic chaplains fell far short of that allowed by Government, and the work became very heavy. Mr. Woolett had toiled day and almost night that none should suffer from the deficiency in number. Passages were taken in the "Ottawar," and preparations were made for the departure of the Sisters. The first week in October was a very busy one, for the General Hospital was to be given over to the Sardinians. Two days before the Sisters left, the patients were moved into Upper Stable Ward (one of the new wards of the Barrack Hospital), stores and furniture were packed up and sent to the purveyor, and numerous packages prepared for the Sisters.

It was necessary they should take a number of things with them, for the accounts from Balaclava were so various. Some said nothing could be had there without paying an enormous price. Mr. Woolett said it was not so, but he had an unusual affection for the camp, and as we feared he made the *best* of things whilst others made the *worst*, it was determined therefore that they should take the middle course.

At length all was ready, and October the 8th was fixed for their departure. Lighters had been ordered to come down from Scutari to take the luggage, but none appeared. At eleven the Sisters could delay no longer, for fear of losing their passage ; they ordered as many boxes as possible to be placed in the caiques, which were to convey them to the Golden Horn, where the " Ottawar " was lying.

The long train of Sisters descended the hill and entered the barrack-yard. They stopped at the extra store-room to bid farewell to our superintendent and the other ladies. The tears came to our eyes as we parted from them. From first to last the utmost cordiality had subsisted between all the ladies and Sisters, and some of us felt we were parting from tried and warm friends.

Passing down to the quay they were again stopped by the number of patients, orderlies, and soldiers from the detachment, crowding to say good-bye, and shower down a last blessing on the heads of those who had been so long their nurses and comforters. The quay was crowded with soldiers and officers; every one in the hospital was sorry they were going, for their simple holy lives had won the respect and goodwill of all.

They embarked in caiques, and were soon on board the " Ottawar." Among their fellow passengers was one going to the camp, whose departure all deeply regretted. Mr. Coney, the senior Church of England chaplain, was ordered to the station of St. George's monastery, and to our real sorrow he quitted us. Our only consolation was that he would have a wider field of work in which to do good ; very much indeed had he done at Koulali, and among those who differed from him in religion, as well as those who agreed with him, he was universally respected and beloved.

I took my last farewell of the Sisters on board the "Ottawar." There I met and was kindly greeted by Miss Nightingale, who was also going up in the "Ottawar," with two nurses, to the Castle Hospital, Balaclava. The Sisters of Mercy, from the General Hospital, Scutari, also here joined their Superioress and the rest of their community, as the whole number were to proceed together to Balaclava.

The General Hospital, Koulali, was closed formally the next day, and the Sardinians were daily expected. Days passed into weeks, and yet no signs of their arrival. The departure of the Sisters made a terrible blank; we could not bear to go near the General Hospital, where we had spent so many happy hours—now gone for ever. General Storks expressed his sorrow at their valuable services being lost to the hospitals in his

command. The medical officers spoke in the
highest terms of the assistance they had rendered while under their orders. One of
them inquired into the peculiar rules of their
order. He had never met with nuns before,
and fancied all religious orders were cloistered,
of which life he said he did not approve, but
thought an active order like this most useful.

Invalids were sent home after the Sisters'
departure, so that our numbers diminished
more and more, while twice a week as usual
a number of men were discharged for duty
while none came down from the camp. We
had now only one hundred men in the Barrack Hospital, and another one hundred
and ten in the Convalescent Hospital, who
were not under our care. We began seriously to contemplate the advisability of
some of our party returning home, as it was
evident that the closing of the General Hospital and the diminution of patients had
more than counterbalanced the loss of the

Sisters, and our staff was far too large for our present work.

Those who had important duties at home, and who had left them only because they were called out by a great emergency, did not feel justified in remaining when that emergency had passed.

One had almost made up her mind to leave when an alteration in the routine at once caused her and others also finally to decide on returning to England. Dr. Humphrey had for some time past considered that the health of the patients had so amended, and the facility of procuring things from the purveyor's stores was so great, that he thought the old routine of the diet-roll ought again to be revived.

An act of disobedience of one of the hired nurses brought matters to a crisis, and Dr. Humphrey issued general orders to the effect that nothing was to be given except from the diet-rolls. This order came so suddenly

that we were dismayed by it. It was issued
to all on November 2nd, and carried into
effect with military rapidity. The ladies'
plans of nursing were upset, and they did
not know what to do with themselves, so
they assembled in the store-room, looking
very blank, and complaining to our superintendent. The lady in charge of the store-
room, who had been thinking of going home,
now laughingly declared the matter was
settled, for her work was done.

In a few days the ladies saw the reason-
ableness of Dr. Humphrey's regulation—
hospital routine had been infringed upon for
many months. The infringement began at
a time of distress unknown in the annals of
military hospitals; it had been carried on
beyond that period, and the time for its dis-
continuance had arrived.

A regulation once made for a military hospital should not be broken. If it is not sufficient for the wants of the men it should be

altered; if it is sufficient it should be obeyed. However, one evident conclusion arose from this change. Some of us must return home, leaving a sufficient staff for the hospital should it ever happen (which was unlikely) to be full again. The numbers then at Koulali exceeded this.

Five of the lady volunteers sent in their resignations to General Storks. He accepted them in the kindest manner, regretting our intended departure, but agreeing that our decision was a wise one.

The superintendent being among those who resigned another was appointed, who was Sister Anne, the only volunteer lady remaining. There was, however, some rumour of the Barrack Hospital now being emptied of patients and given up to the German legion, for whom room was wanted. General Storks did not wish to do this, as he thought the landing place at Koulali so convenient for the sick in the rough weather which was ex-

pected in the winter, but he had to suspend
his decision till he could communicate with
the Government at home; he therefore requested our superintendent to remain in office
till this point was decided.

The other three ladies and myself were set
at liberty, and able to enjoy some of the
wonderful sights of the East ere we returned
to England. We much regretted that our
superintendent could not accompany us,
especially as she had never, save on two
visits of business to Lady Stratford, left the
hospital during her stay in it.

CHAPTER XII.

OUR first visit was to the far-famed bazaars of Stamboul. The contrast of shopping there to shopping in Pera is striking. You hardly ever meet a Frank in Stamboul; none are permitted to reside there.

Disembarking at Galata we traversed the bridge, and on reaching the Stamboul side were assailed by a group of worthies who called themselves interpreters—their knowledge of the English and French languages ranging from twelve to twenty words, but who were able to supply all deficiencies by their abundant use of signs. In an evil hour does an unfortunate traveller engage one of these gentlemen to attend him. The presence of one entails upon you that of a dozen—they declare they are all "brothers"—and they follow you about like a pack of dogs. They only allow you to buy at the shops they select, and at all these they have an understanding with the shopkeepers by which they get a per centage on all you may happen to buy. They do not allow you to speak; they surround you, and shout in their own languages a mixture of Greek, Turkish and Armenian, till your head fairly swims, and you are willing to buy the article at any price to escape from the noise.

Both Greeks and Turks always talk as loud as we should shout, and jabber and gesticulate so as to make you think they are on the point of proceeding to blows; but they are quite calm in reality all the time. When we grew wiser, and came to Stamboul with our own interpreters, it was a delight to walk through the bazaars. True, they are dark and dirty, narrow, and paved as badly as the streets of Pera, but one could fancy oneself transported back to the days of one's childhood, and that the scenes described in the "Arabian Nights," to which we listened with rapt attention, were now realised.

Here were the embroidered slippers, pipes, divans, rich stuffs, bright colours, and all the wonders which one's fancy had painted. Here were the jewellers and the charm-makers, and here were Damascus scarves and

Broussa silks, and glittering table covers and
bags, and tobacco pouches of every shade of
colour and richly embroidered, and here at
the corners of the streets were the tables of
the money-changers. Here instead of count-
ers were the divans whereon the Turk sat
quietly and smoked his chibouque, and did
you wish to make a bargain you sat down
also on the divan, and gravely, by means of
your interpreter, discussed the subject. You
fix perhaps on a pair of Turkish slippers
which the interpreter advises you to give
thirty piastres (five shillings) for. You say
"katch grosh?" (how much?) the Turk
informs you it is one hundred piastres; the
interpreter says "Mashallah!" throws up
his hands, and laughs scornfully. The Turk
does the same. You rise to go and proceed
on your way, but are suddenly recalled and
told you may have it for the thirty piastres.

It has a singular effect to look down the
streets of the bazaars and see each long row

of divans entirely furnished with one particular article. One street of embroidered slippers, another fezs, another bags, another jewellery, another cashmeres, and so on. The extreme brilliance, richness of colour of the Turkish manufactures adds much to the effect. The cashmere bazaar is beautiful. The blue and geranium colours are unequalled in their peculiar richness of colour, while the soft texture of the materials exceeds all European manufactures, which is the reason why the dresses of a group of Turkish women fail to produce the gaudy effect which such a variety of colours would have in England. They always dress in one colour, but in a group one will be in blue, another in green, another in geranium, another in orange, another in yellow, another in lavender, and the colouring of each is so exquisite that they *en masse* look more like a bed of flowers than anything else.

At times the bazaars are much crowded,
and many Turkish ladies may be seen, for
shopping appears to be their great amusement.   Turkish carriages filled with ladies
occasionally pass through the bazaars, oblig-
ing the foot passengers to climb on to the
divan to escape being trodden down.

Here and there vendors of lemonade offer
refreshing draughts to the weary traveller.
Then, again, in small white saucers, is a
dainty, somewhat resembling blanc-mange,
which the Turks seem to consider very in-
viting ; then tables and trays full of pistachio
nuts, chesnuts, and almond cakes can be
found ; but if any other refreshment is
needed the traveller must wend his way to
Pera, for he will not get it in Stamboul.

Now we come to the chibouque bazaar,
and find pipes of every variety ; the cherry-
stick, either rough or polished, or richly
painted, the amber mouth-pieces of all sizes
—the imitation amber and the commoner

kind of pipes. Then there are the shops, in which all sorts of nicknacks are to be bought; the beautiful amber-bead chaplets, the same of red Jerusalem-beads; also sandal-wood, with its sweet scent. Almost every Turk one meets carries in his hand a chaplet, or string of beads in three divisions —thirty beads in each division, and divided off by larger beads—the whole finished with a long shoot of the same material as the beads. Then there are the pastiles, wrapped in gold leaf, one of which is sometimes put into the chibouque to add to the fragrance of the tobacco; the coffee cup-holders, in chased silver or carved wood; the tiny coffee cups themselves of china. The bracelet chains, and little bags made of pressed rose leaves, coloured black. These are the leaves of the roses after the attar has been pressed out of them. Then there is the celebrated attar itself, and scents of all kinds, of which our interpreter seemed to think the English were

very fond, as he always invited us to buy
them, and was much surprised if we refused.
Then there are the little boxes of henna and
black paint, with which the Turkish women
stain their finger-nails and colour their eye-
brows and eyelashes; and the " mastic,"
which they constantly chew, in order to add
to the whiteness of their teeth.

Next come the large Turkish fans, some
made of straw, and the more expensive ones of
peacocks' feathers, with a small looking-glass
in the centre.   The principal amusement of
the ladies in the carriages seemed to be sur-
veying themselves in this glass, arranging
their yashmacs, which were sometimes made
of extremely fine transparent muslin, especially when there was a beautiful face underneath.   Some of the cheaper fans, made of
common feathers or straw, we found very
useful in the hospitals during the summer.

Then there is the literary bazaar, where the
Turk sits cross-legged, looking very grave

and very wise, writing and transcribing
Turkish characters, which we did not understand, but were struck with the look of superior intelligence and extreme interest displayed on the faces of those thus engaged.
Next the jewellers' bazaar, of which they
seem very proud. They think a great deal of
jewellery, at least to judge from the quantity
the ladies wear both on their hands and
heads. The lower class of women also are
seldom seen without a large jewelled ring on
their finger, or brooch to fasten their yashmacs. Then there is the tobacco, which is
so much prized in England, and which is less
than half the price, I believe, in Turkey,
owing to the high duty to which it is subject
in this country.

There are also the sweetmeat shops, principally outside the bazaars, looking very gay
with their bright-coloured bon-bons, candied
sugar, and white and rose-coloured arrachle-
comb, which is the principal Turkish sweet-

meat, and of which it is reported the Sultan's ladies eat so much that he rather complains of the expense.   It is a sort of sweet gummy substance, with either pistachio nuts or almonds stuck into it, and it is somewhat expensive.   The Turks sell this and the tobacco, and several other things, by the " ock," which is about two and a half pounds English weight.   The Turkish weights are different to ours, their pound being about twelve ounces.   The currency is chiefly in paper. There are two notes—one ten piastres, another twenty.   There are also gold and silver pieces, but these are seldom used.   Bracelets are made of the Turkish silver or gold coins.   The Turks always prefer English money, and in making a bargain inquire whether you will pay in English money.

Passing through the bazaars we soon came to the building called the epitaph of Sultan Mahmoud.   It is a circular one, and contains his tomb, of which we only gained a

sight by peeping through the windows.
The tomb is richly ornamented with sculpture,
and beside it we saw an imaum in prayer.
Within the outer enclosure is a garden, in
which is a fountain of water, with iron cups
fastened to it, so that all who choose may
drink.   These fountains are generally found
outside in all large mosques, providing water
for the poor being considered a religious duty,
and a great boon it must be to the poor Turks
in the parching heat of summer.

Among the most curious sights of Constantinople are the aqueducts.   The first of these
is Yere Batan Serai, intended to supply the
city with water in case of a siege, as the
soil of Constantinople does not produce
drinkable water; the water is conveyed to it
from Belgrade, or rather the great aqueducts
six miles from that town, the arches of which
can be seen in the distance from Buyukdere.
Yere Batan Serai, or the swallowed-up
palace, is one of the most remarkable con-

structions ever known. It would appear
that nearly the whole of Constantinople is
undermined with it, for none can ever
discover its extent; different parts of the
roof have fallen in, and three accidents have
occurred at quarters of the city miles distant
from each other. All these cisterns must have
been built in the first two centuries after the
foundation of the city. The roof of the
mysterious water-palace is supported by
marble pillars, each formed of a single
block.

Bin Vebir Direg, or cistern of the thou-
sand and one, is the next object of interest.
The name implies that the roof is supported
by 1,001 columns, but in reality there are
but 336. There were three stories to this
cistern, though but one is now accessible; it
has been reckoned that when these three
stories were full they alone contained sufficient water for the whole number of inhabitants of Constantinople for ten or twelve

days. The columns are formed of several blocks, and the marble is much coarser than that of Yere Batan Serai; narrow windows closely grated and built near the roof admit the light. The cistern is entirely filled up. When Signor Fossati was repairing Santa Sophia some years since, the soil taken out was thrown into Bin Vebir Direg and the water courses turned off. The immense space thus left vacant is overspread by silk-workers.

Descending a ladder we found ourselves in this mysterious subterranean palace; wending in and out among the columns were the long lines of silk, which we could just distinguish in the dim light, looking like magic threads; while the strange beings at the works, with their pale faces (for the atmosphere is most unhealthy), their rapid movements at their weaving, and the shrill tones of their voices shrieking to us not to injure their silk, which the hollow echoes repeated, made the scene a most unearthly one. The air was so stifling that we hastened to quit this horrible place, but before doing so were assailed by a group of the wild, haggard-looking silk-workers catching our clothes and begging vociferously for "backshish." We were indeed thankful to gain the open air.

At a short distance from the seraglio a Greek gentleman, who was kindly escorting us, stopped at the door of a large building guarded by sentries; there was a little demur as to our admittance, but the sight of the uniform of an English officer, also of our party, and a little additional backshish, as usual carried the day, and the door flew open. Upon entering I started back, for just before me stood a Turk of enormous stature, fierce countenance, and threatening gesture. A burst of laughter from the sentry reassured me, and I discovered the fierce-looking figure before me was made of plaster.

We then entered a large hall, from which four rooms opened, and we found ourselves in a Turkish "Madame Tussaud's."   All round these rooms were glass cases, in which were ranged hundreds of plaster or painted wooden figures larger than life.   About in the hall these figures were placed in groups; they were mostly arrayed in the warlike costumes worn by the different regiments of the once famous Janissaries, and were put there by order of Sultan Mahmoud, who after he had succeeded in destroying this formidable body of men was anxious that their dress should be perpetuated.   One specimen of the dress of each regiment was here, and the effect of the many varieties of costume was curious enough.   The artist had succeeded admirably in his work, for the various countenances of these gaunt figures gave us a complete idea of the fierce race they were intended to represent.

Besides those of the Janissaries there was a

representation of each minister of state and
the principal imaums. The turbans of some of
the figures were very singular, consisting of
rolls of white calico twisted till they were
five feet high; others had high felt hats,
either square or conical, about four feet high.
One case contained very different figures;
they were made of wax, and were representations of Circassian or Georgian women,
probably some beauties of the Sultan's harem.
Their soft complexions and beautiful, though
unintellectual faces, formed a strong contrast
to the ferocious warriors around them.

We were struck by the evidence afforded
of the Sultan Mahmoud's bold infraction of the
command in the Koran, forbidding all human
representations.   There was something extremely painful in this sight.   The figures,
though so rude, had a horrible lifelike look :
the fierce eyes seemed to glare at one, and it
was with a sensation of extreme relief that
we quitted the Elbicei Atika.

The Atmeidan, or ancient hippodrome lies behind the seraglio. Here is all that remains now of ancient Byzantium, the obelisk of Theodosius, and the serpentine column. The last is inscribed with hieroglyphics : it is supposed to be at least 3,000 years old. The serpentine column consisted of three serpents entwined, all of which have lost their heads long ago. It is nearly in ruins, and the base sunk into the earth. Its origin is quite uncertain. Some suppose Constantine caused it to be transported from Delphos, but this is not authenticated.

One great interest will ever attach itself to the great plain of the Atmeidan, for here took place the massacre of the Janissaries by Sultan Mahmoud. For long years the sultans of Turkey had groaned under the yoke of these oppressors. The Janissaries were so powerful a body that they set all laws at defiance, and virtually ruled the empire. The reforms wrought by Sultan

Mahmoud gave them such displeasure that endless seditions were fostered by them. At length an open rebellion burst forth; they overturned their soup-kettles, and threatened to fire the city. (The Janissaries when marching carried before each regiment a large soup-kettle instead of a standard.) And assembled at their barracks, situated at one end of the Atmeidan.

The brave Sultan summoned the few troops on whom he could depend, and headed them himself. The battle began. The Janissaries retreated into their barracks, and there the fight turned into a massacre; for the Sultan's troops set fire to the buildings and all were consumed. About 5000 Janissaries perished on that day, and the troop was extinct. The Sultan's vengeance was not sated till the turban on the tomb of every deceased Janissary was knocked off, and many of their decapitated monuments are to be seen in the great cemeteries.

Near the Atmerda stands the Mosque of
Sultan Achmet. Its chief beauty consists in
the colossal proportions of the four columns
which support the whole weight of the building. Turkish relics, highly valued by the nation, are kept here, but not exposed to view.
Like most mosques, it was without furniture
or decorations.

On the last Friday we spent in the East we
intended to have seen the dancing dervishes,
and went to Galata for that purpose; but,
to our great disappointment, the Armenian
gentleman who had promised to escort us,
informed us on our arrival that a fire the
previous night had burnt the Tehle or
dervishes' house to the ground. They
would not therefore dance until the following Friday; and before that day arrived we
had left the East.

As we could not visit the dervishes, we
proceeded to the French hospital at Pera.
Our kind Armenian friend had procured for

us the only two carriages with springs to be
hired in Pera.   We drove to the hospital,
which is distant about two miles from Pera..
This building is a very fine one, admirably
adapted for an hospital.   We proceeded to the
apartments occupied by the *Sœurs de la
Charité*, twelve of whom are attached to this
hospital.   By them we were conducted
through the wards—they were nearly empty.

Those who were wounded in the assault
of Sebastopol had recovered, and from fif-
teen hundred the numbers had been reduced
to five hundred.

We had long been anxious to visit this hospital, having heard much of it from our very
first arrival in the East.   During the time of
distress in our own hospitals it had been
spoken of in high terms as possessing all we
then so much needed.   This was probably
the case, but many months had passed, and
now certainly we had outstripped our allies
in the appearance of our hospital.   How-

ever, it must be considered that during the summer, while *our* hospitals were empty, *theirs* had been crowded. The wards for both officers and men were inferior in cleanliness and general appearance of comfort to those at Koulali and Scutari, but of the management and routine of the French hospital we had, of course, no means of judging.

From Pera we drove to the castle of the Seven Towers, or the old state prison where captives were immured under charge of the Janissaries. Even foreign ambassadors were among these prisoners when war was declared against the countries they represented; for the Turks in those days did not think it worth while to keep faith with Christians. Times are changed indeed when the empire would be lost were not Christian blood shed to defend it. An older and sadder history even than theirs still clings to these now ruined walls. Beneath them was fought the last battle between the Ottomans and Greeks; there the Cross

fell before the Crescent, and from that vic-
torious battle-field Mahomet II. rode into
the city.

The ruins of the Seven Towers had till
lately long been deserted and silent, but
busy sounds were once more heard among
them. One of the numerous French hospitals
was erected among the ruins, which are fast
falling into utter decay. This hospital consisted entirely of huts, which were neatly
built and had every appearance of comfort.
The wards were beautifully clean, far more
so than the stone ones at Pera. We saw
one hut raised on a mound of earth. On
entering we found it was the extra diet
kitchen, furnished with a charcoal stove and
boilers; the flooring being the uncovered
ground. Several soldiers were very busy
cooking, and a Sister of Charity superintend-
ing. In the centre of this hut was an immense space, boarded round and covered
with planks. On inquiry we found it was

an old well, into which the Janissaries were wont to throw some victims of their vengeance. Some of the boards were removed to allow us to look down, and the soldiers took brands from the fire and cast them into it that we might see by the glare, as they descended, the fearful depth, and the water at the bottom; one brief look was quite sufficient, and the boarding was replaced.

At this moment the French principal medical officer of the hospital entered to give some directions to the *Sœur*, and taste the soup, &c., which she was preparing for the patients. We were struck by the extreme courtesy of his manner to her, for although she was evidently not a lady either by birth or education, her office inspired more respect than if she had possessed both. The French doctor spoke courteously to us, expressing his pleasure at our visit to his hospital. Three huts were set apart for the Sisters' use, a fourth formed the chapel. There were at least one hundred huts altogether. They appeared so securely built that we were astonished to hear from *Madame la Supérieure* that the rain came through in torrents, so that in wet weather the inhabitants were obliged to sleep under umbrellas.

The Seven Towers were built on the summit of a hill, and exquisite is the view which lay stretched before the eyes of the poor captives who spent their weary days within their walls—how they must have pined to be beside the blue Bosphorus breathing the free air of heaven!

After leaving the castle we drove about a mile further on, and arrived at the summit of the hill above Bebek, which is so steep that the carriages could not descend without injuring their springs; so we left them there, walked down the hill, and crossed to Koulali in caiques. The drive from Pera to the Seven Towers is one of the few that can be taken in a European carriage, as the ground is tolerably level for some miles, but the country around is very barren and uninteresting.

CHAPTER XIII.

THERE is one spot in Constantinople to
which the heart of the Christian must ever
turn with the most intense interest. Old Roman and Byzantine remains, subterranean
palaces, records of the ferocious Janissaries

all fade away into nothingness as we approach the door of Agia Sophia (the Church of the Eternal Wisdom). This great edifice stands at the north of the Atmeidan, on an elevated ridge; the northern end of which ridge reaches to Seraglio Point.

Close by Santa Sophia once stood the great palace of the Cæsars, divided from it only by the forum of Augustus, which formed a common entrance to both church and palace. The gardens and terraces of the palace of the Cæsars must have extended from the ridge on which Santa Sophia was built to the seashore. We stood before Santa Sophia at the principal entrance through which the Sultan had entered on the Beiram. Here we were positively refused admittance.

We then proceeded to a side entrance, and on passing within the porch descended a flight of stone steps and found ourselves in a portico amid a host of imaums. A few yards from us was a door covered only with carpet hangings. To our left was another small door, made in the wall, closely locked. Here ensued the usual quarrel with imaums about backshish.

I paid several visits to Santa Sophia, but shall condense all that I saw and learnt about it in one account. At these different visits we paid various sums for admission; at the time of Ramazan it was very high, and there was a great uproar before we gained admittance; we then paid one hundred piastres for a large party, at other times we paid less.

At length this knotty point was settled; one of the imaums opened the door in the wall and made us follow him, carefully locking it behind him. A winding inclined plane led us up to the women's gallery; in the centre of this are raised some wooden steps, ascending which we obtained a more extensive view of the church.

The first feeling is that of admiration at the vastness of this wonderful building, and not the least part of this wonder is that the whole extent of the dome flashes on one at the first glance.   One does not have to wait, as it is said people do, when they enter St. Peter's at Rome, to calculate the vastness; for there, I have heard it is not till you walk under the dome you see it to advantage. Standing on the threshold of Santa Sophia one sees the whole extent of the dome as well as the greater part of the interior at a glance.

Santa Sophia as a mosque possesses neither ornament nor decoration of any kind, save a number of immense green shields engraven in gold, with sentences from the Koran, which are hung upon the pillars covering the capitals; a number of silver lamps are also hung around.   The Nimber and Mihrab or desk, from which the Koran is read, stands in that part which was once the chancel.   Opposite to this a gilded throne for the Sultan; an old carpet hangs at the east end, its only value consisting in its having come from Mecca, and this is all.

Great care has the Mussulman taken to hide every token of the former possessors of Santa Sophia ; the flooring is covered thickly with matting—plaster has hidden the mosaic walls and roof. A few Turks, both men and women, were prostrating themselves on the matting, and the monotonous howl in which they pray was echoed up to the gallery, sounding almost like the cry of evil spirits. The imaums in the gallery eagerly pressed us to buy some little bits of mosaic which they are always pulling down from the walls to sell.

And this was Santa Sophia in 1855, but thought would not rest here. This was no mosque like Sultan Achmet's, which one entered only to admire marble pillars and vast proportions. This was a Christian church, however desecrated. It was once the especial dwelling of the Lord of hosts, and memory carried one away into those far off years to trace the history of Santa Sophia,

and treasure up its wondrous annals. We
thought of its first building by Constantine,
in 326. Although this building—which was
supposed to be of wood—was destroyed by
fire, the present church stands on the exact
site of the ancient one, and in the gallery
parts of the pillars of the first building have
been used in constructing the second, so that
all the memories which cling to the church
built by Constantine attach themselves to the
work of Justinian, and we gazed down from
the gallery and tried to forget the present
scene and the false worship while the visions
of the past rose up before the mind's eye. To
follow the whole of that long history would
be impossible, but there are some scenes
written indelibly upon its pages.

Thought transports one back 1400 years.
The vast church is filled with an eager
multitude; the women's gallery is crowded
with noble ladies : among them sits the Empress Eudoxia, in all her pomp. The sounds

of Christian worship ring through those old walls; bishops, priests, and deacons stand around, and now rises one from amidst their number—a man whose pale face tells the tale of fast and vigil, and how in solitude he learned the secret of that wonderful eloquence which shall make the heart of that great multitude quiver as one man.   Yes, there he stands upon the altar steps, a man low in stature but great in soul, the patriarch of Constantinople, St. John Chrysostom.

And now he speaks, and awestruck they all listen to those words of fire.   Are they words of burning warning that he is pouring forth, or are they those addresses of ardent love, in which he told them that he would lose his sight for their sakes, because sweeter to him than all the sights of this fair world was the salvation of their souls ?* and as he pauses there is a stir in the vast assembly. According to the custom of the age their ad-

* Life of St. Chrysostom.

miration bursts forth—they wave their garments and plumes, lay hands upon their swords and shout, "Worthy the priesthood: thirteenth apostle, Christ hath sent thee."*

But these sounds of praise—generally liked by the preachers of those days—had no effect on that stern spirit. He knew the world's applause was fleeting, and bids his hearers show, not by words of acclamation but by tears, of penitence, that he had touched their hearts, and he judged well. Not long was Santa Sophia to be filled with admiring crowds, not long did the haughty empress listen to his fervid words—truth was not palatable to that luxurious court.

The scene is changed, no longer do they listen within the church and bend before the altar; they who had praised him rose up against him and drove him into exile. He crossed over to Asia, but his foes did not triumph long. A violent earthquake shook the city, and the affrighted people thought it was a

* " Characteristics of Men of Genius."

judgment upon them for the sin of his banishment. They sent messengers to recall him, the whole city went out to meet him. The Bosphorus was bridged across with boats, and lighted up with torches. Two short months passed by, while he prayed and preached within Santa Sophia's walls, when the storm of persecution recommenced.

A silver statue of the empress was placed before Santa Sophia's doors, and around it the people danced and feasted, and sounds of the wild revelry of a great multitude pierced through the wall and drowned the songs of praise. Chrysostom thundered forth his stern rebuke, though knowing that bitter persecution would be his portion, fearlessly the bishop denounced their impiety, and now the empress was resolved on a lasting vengeance. Santa Sophia's floor was stained with blood, for the emperor's troops came even on Easter eve, the day of all the year of holy calm, to drive the people from the church where St. Chrysostom is ministering.

A few weeks of struggle pass away—when the songs of Whitsuntide should be ringing through the church, there are instead sounds of weeping and mourning.   Can we not fancy we see him now before the high altar in Santa Sophia, praying the Eternal Wisdom to direct his steps?

They bring in the sentence of his banishment.   No more must he teach the flock, for whose salvation he had so yearned ; that tongue whose eloquence the world has never equalled, was to be stilled for ever.   Perhaps before his eyes floated some vision of the woe which was to fall over the city, and desecrate his loved cathedral.

Around him gather his bishops, and when he parted from them his last words were, as if in prophecy, "Farewell to the angel of this church."   Embracing them with tears, and blessing the deaconesses who flocked around him, and in touching words entreating that they would offer up prayers for their exiled bishop, and then avoiding the attention of the multitude, he went to his doom—to wander three years in the wilderness, dragged about by brutal guards—rest at night—clean water to drink, bread to eat were often denied to him whom once in Santa Sophia the people almost worshipped. No murmur passed the saintly lips—they led him through the scorching heats which poured down their fury on that bald head—they led him out in rains till he was drenched in streams of water. At last the hour of release was at hand; he asks for rest, for he knows death is near; the guards only drag him on more violently than before. But there is a Power stronger than they. At last they are forced to lay him in a roadside chapel, and there he called for the white garments of his priesthood, and saying in death that which had been his song through life, "Glory be to God for all things," went to his rest.

Thus died the great Patriarch of Constantinople; his memory is the principal interest which attaches to the former church of Santa Sophia.

In 532 this temple was laid in ruins by fire. Justinian then sat on the throne. He was a great man, and he conceived the mighty ambition to build a church which should excel the temple of Solomon. The foundation of it was laid forty days after the fire. In less than six years his work was completed, and Justinian beholding it, exclaimed, "Solomon, I have conquered thee!"

During the reign of this emperor an earthquake did great damage to the church. Its ravages were, however, perfectly restored, and for 1300 years, though countless earthquakes have shaken the city, not one has touched Santa Sophia. Against fire Justinian carefully preserved it, for he ordered his builders to employ fire-proof materials; this has been carried out even to the doors and

windows—the tracery work of the windows is
of stone and the doors either of bronze or
covered with it. Some of the windows, it is
said, contain panes of the oldest glass ever
made, but the date of their insertion is unknown. In the apse of the eastern windows
are inner windows of coloured glass, which
the Turks allow to remain as a curiosity.
The Imaums drew our attention to these, and
pointed them out with evident pride. The
door frames are of bright-coloured marble,
except that which was the emperor's entrance-
door, and which was of bronze. Over all
the doors are large hooks, or rings, as it was
customary to suspend hangings or veils
before the church door. This is now a
universal custom in the Greek churches;
the door curtain is always made of some
heavy material, with bars of wood placed in
it, so that it is difficult to lift. The emperor's entrance-door is adorned with a bas
relief, it consists of an arch supported by

columns; beneath is a throne, over which is
the Holy Ghost as a dove descending from
heaven, holding in the beak the book of the
Gospel, having written outside "I am the
door of the sheep."

The other doors were not remarkable
except those at the south end; these are of
planks of timber, four or five times thick,
covered with bronze. The ornamental work
of the door is so graceful and beautiful that
it is supposed to belong to the most brilliant
time of Grecian art.

Sculpture was not much thought of in the
way of ornament in Santa Sophia, save in the
employment of rare and costly marbles,
these were brought together by Justinian
from every quarter of his vast empire.
Whole walls in the interior and the porches
were covered with these magnificent materials from floor to cornice; masses of
bright colours were arranged in stripes, and
bands, and patterns, interspersed with white.

We left the women's gallery and descending the winding passage found ourselves once more in the portico.   Another uproar ensued before we were suffered to cross the threshold.   We were obliged to take off our shoes, and then the curtain was lifted and in a moment we found ourselves on the floor of the far-famed temple.   The *coup d' œil* was marvellous; from arch to arch as one glances up to the stupendous height of the dome— what must it not have been in the days of its glory and beauty!   There have been some fortunate enough within the last few years to have gained some idea of it, for in 1847, the present Sultan being alarmed that Santa Sophia was falling to decay, determined on a complete repair, and engaged the services of Signor Fossati, the celebrated Italian architect, by whom it was most successfully accomplished.   During this restoration the marble of the floor, the mosaic, and other beauties were uncovered; and the Sultan

even allowed them to be copied, stipulating
only that they should be re-covered, as
contrary to the law of the Koran.

Upon Santa Sophia Justinian and his
successors poured every imaginable splendour
—the old idol temples were ransacked of
their ancient treasures for this purpose—
they brought the dark red porphyry from
the Temple of the Sun at Rome, and dark
green from Thessaly for the columns, while
the cornices were of white marble, and on
the white they carved the palm leaf in deep
relief, covering it with gold. The pillars
standing near the emperor's public entrance
were carved with four white doves, with pas-
sion-flower and cross between ; the flooring
was all of costly marble; the nave and women's
gallery of white and grey, the rest of
bright colours, all bordered with verd
antique. But the great beauty of all was
the mosaic. Walls and roof were covered
with it ; the whole grounding was of gold, the

pictures of saints and angels, groups of flowers, or holy emblems in colours.

Silver mosaic was largely used, and it is believed to have been almost the only church in the world where it was so. The gold and silver mosaic had a peculiar character—it was of glass mosaic, an art of which the Byzantines were masters. On the roof of Santa Sophia thin plates of glass were first fixed with cement, the gold laid upon it, and then covered with a similar plate of glass; it is therefore almost imperishable. Neither the dust of ages nor the whitewashing efforts of the Turks have destroyed its brilliancy.

The most splendid mosaic in the church is that over the Emperor's entrance—the representation of the Agia Sophia himself. He is enthroned in glory, His robes are of white and gold, His right hand lifted up as if in the act of speaking; in the left the gospels, on which is written "I am the light of the

world." At His feet is prostrated the
Emperor, clad in his diadem and regal robes,
of blue, red, and gold, in the act meant to
represent a vassal doing homage to his liege
lord. This is supposed to be Justinian himself. On each side of our Lord are medal-
lions of the Mother of God and the archangel Michael.

On the roof of the women's gallery is a
representation of the Day of Pentecost. On
the west end are figures of the Blessed
Virgin, St. Peter, and St. Paul. These are
not in good preservation, for the figure of
the Holy Child, which was placed with His
Mother, is gone—only the crown of glory
left. Around this picture is a rainbow.

On the walls are numbers of pictures of
bishops and martyrs, and also of six lesser
and two greater prophets. Isaiah is holding
a scroll with the words—"A virgin shall
conceive and bear a child;" and with his
right hand he points to the sanctuary. There

are also the cherubims with their six wings, and other pictures in profusion. The centre picture of the dome is supposed to have been Christ as the Judge of the world, but it is gone.

The rood screen had twelve columns and three doors. Over it stood an archangel with gleaming sword to guard the holy place. The covering and ornaments of the altar were all of gold. The ciborium with silver pillars and veil of rich embroidery; on it hovered the dove, typical of the Holy Ghost.

The holy vessels themselves were one blaze of precious stones. When one reads and ponders over the account of all the splendour of this church, which surely must have been the glory of Christendom, we enter into the feelings of its old historian, who said—" When one once puts a foot in Santa Sophia one desires never to depart from it."

Again the vision of those old times floats before our sight.   One stands in Santa Sophia upon that marble floor, under the shade of that great dome, the candelabra and crowns of light shed their rays on gold and silver, and pictured forms ; forth comes the long procession, the many bishops, the sixty priests, the hundred deacons, and other officers, altogether four hundred and twenty-five who served this church*—they come to adore the Eternal Wisdom.

> " Anthems soaring loud ;
> Incense curled up and wreathed on high a cloud ;
> And all tongues choired adoring cup and host—
> Glory to Father, Son, and Holy Ghost."†

But those days have long since passed ; the glory of Santa Sophia was perchance too much for this poor earth—it did not linger

* Besides this large number were 100 door-keepers. It is, however, recorded in the old histories of Santa Sophia, that its clergy served three other churches— the church of the Mother of God, that of the Martyr Theodore, and also that of St. Irene.

† Moile.

long. The church of Constantinople was
rent, Chrysostom's prophecy was fulfilled—
the angel departed from it.

Storms and dissensions shake the city,
the sound of woe is in the air; beneath
the Seven Towers the Greeks resist the in-
vaders. In a side chapel, near the women's
gallery, in Santa Sophia, an old priest is saying mass; they bring him news that all is
lost. He believes them not. At last the
sound of horses' hoofs is heard, Mahomet
II., flushed with victory, rides into Santa
Sophia, and, dashing his hand, stained with
Christian blood, upon the walls, proclaims its
fall. The old priest pauses. The Turks
rush upon him, but the wall of the chapel
opening he passes in carrying the holy vessels. They tried to break down the wall, but
no power could move a stone. The Greeks
aver that occasionally through the walls come
faint sounds of psalmody, and when at length
the time of their captivity shall be past,

and Santa Sophia be restored to God's service,
the wall shall re-open of itself, the priest—
who is now sleeping and chanting in his sleep
—shall come forth and finish the interrupted
mass.   Thus runs the old legend.

As we once more looked around and realised the sad knowledge that the Mussulman
desecrated the holy walls of Santa Sophia,
earnest was the prayer we silently breathed
that God would once more come to His temple,
and that the wonderful events of the last few
years might be instrumental in paving the way
for the restoration of this beautiful cathedral
to its former holy purposes.   We prayed the
time might hasten on when the white robes
shall gleam as of old, the floor shall be covered with worshippers among the faithful,
and those old walls which have seen Em-
perors, Sultans, and dynasties flourish and
decay through so many centuries shall again
re-echo with the song of praise,—*Te Deum
laudamus.*

Near Santa Sophia stands the old church of St. Irene, built by Justinian; razed to the ground, like Santa Sophia, by fire, it was restored by Justinian. It was served by the clergy of Santa Sophia, and shared its title of patriarchal. It was destroyed by an earth-quake in the eighth century, and does not seem to have been restored to its ancient beauty. It is now used by the Turks as a store-house for weapons, and its ecclesiastical remains can only be conjectured. Whatever were its beauties they have now disappeared, but it would seem to have been built upon the plan of Santa Sophia. In the hall, or portico, are deposited some ancient remains of art.

The exterior of Santa Sophia presents nothing worthy of remark; it would appear originally to have had little ornament be-stowed upon it, and under the Turkish rule has lost all. It is disfigured by four minarets, marking its unhallowed use, and all round the church are thrown large buttresses. On the western side is an outer court built of brick, but ornamented internally with marble and mosaic work ; in the centre of this stood a stone vase for water. This court is now occupied by the dwellings of the Imaums, which are built in among the old columns and walls. In place of the ancient holy water vase is the fountain for the Turkish ablutions.

The old baptistery stood at the south-west angle of the church ; it was octagonal, with eight windows and a vaulted roof. It was first converted by the Turks into a store-room for oil, and then at the death of Sultan Mustapha was made his tomb ; there also his brother was buried. It is still used as the tomb of the Sultans, and its memory as the Christian baptistery was utterly lost till Monsieur Salzenberg, in his researches, rescued it

from oblivion.* On the south of Santa
Sophia also stood the oratory of St. John the
Baptist; this was built previous to the time
of Justinian.

* In the account of the details of Santa Sophia, I
have drawn somewhat largely from the work of the
learned Monsieur Salzenberg, Alt Christliche Bandenk-
male von Constantinople, feeling sure that as this valuable work is difficult of access in England any information from it would be acceptable, more especially as
Monsieur Salzenberg enjoyed opportunities of pursuing
his researches in Santa Sophia which will probably
during the period of its restoration by Signor Fossati
again be afforded in our generation.

CHAPTER XIV.

FROM the time the Sisters of Mercy left us
we looked anxiously for letters, and took the

deepest interest in their affairs.   Every one who came down from Balaclava was eagerly questioned concerning them and their work, and all spoke of their exertions in the highest terms.

On their arrival at Balaclava they were lodged in huts built of planks, through the chinks of which the winds whistled cheerlessly.   The hospital consisted partly of huts, partly of a stone building.   Many civilians were nursed in these huts, men from the transport corps, muleteers, &c., who did not receive even the attention paid to the soldiers.

The huts in which the Sisters lived were so bare and unfurnished that they looked like Indian wigwams, but every hardship seemed but to increase the good Sisters' cheerful zeal, they were so delighted at having plenty of work.   They found the character of the work very different from that at Koulali, from patients coming in at all hours, and in a state of acute disease.   Cholera prevailed to some extent in October; the Sisters immediately began night work, and partly owing to the incessant watching many cholera patients recovered.

They had not been many weeks at Balaclava when a sad trial befell them: this was the death of one of the Sisters, the first of their community whom they had lost. After one day's illness with cholera Sister Winifred departed; her death was very peaceful, her Sisters knelt around her bed while the priest recited the prayers for the agonizing; they changed into a requiem, and that was the first token to those who watched that the spirit had fled. Next day, a Sunday afternoon, they bore her to her grave; for this a craggy spot on the hills in view of the huts where the Sisters lived was selected. Priests bearing the cross and chanting led the procession; the coffin was carried by the soldiers for whose sake she had been content to die; the long train of Sisters in white cloaks and bearing tapers followed. Many other people joined them to testify their respect, and so they laid her body in its last resting-place on earth.

The sorrow of the Sisters for their loss did not abate their zeal. One and all were only more anxious rightly to fulfil their appointed work. As time passed on we heard of the improvements they effected. The orderlies at Balaclava had been a troublesome set, unaccustomed to habits of cleanliness and order; reforms were now introduced and carried out : encouragement from the Sisters and their gentle manners did much more good in teaching the orderlies than all the blame they had previously received. Just at this time the corps of civil orderlies, reported to be already trained to undertake nursing arrived from England. They landed at Scutari and were soon dispersed among the other hospitals. They all wore a uniform dress of blue smocks, and were pronounced by the soldiers to be " a set of butchers."

The patients did not at all like losing their
comrades for orderlies, and I do not think the
first few weeks' experience of the "blues"
could have been very gratifying to their feelings. I had no personal experience of them,
but, from what I was told, I fear intemperance
prevailed among this corps of orderlies quite
as much as among the military ones, and
that it was quite as much trouble to train
them to their work. At Balaclava the Sisters appeared to encounter a repetition of
our great discomforts at Koulali—want of
"Etnas," saucepans, &c. They often regretted their nice kitchen at Koulali; but in
course of time their patient perseverance
overcame all difficulties, and at Balaclava
there is now an extra-diet kitchen and store-
room which rival those of the model hospital.

More comfortable huts have been erected for the Sisters, which they speak of
as delightful habitations; and though the
winter's cold must have been intense,
complaints of the unavoidable hardships

never came. When we left the East our last accounts of the Sisters were most satisfactory, their improvements all progressing as well as they could wish. It was pleasing to see the strong interest and affection which continued to be expressed for them after their departure by all at Koulali, and this quite as much so by those who differed from as by those who agreed with them in religion; for all appreciated the gentle courtesy displayed by them to every-one as well as their devotion to their work. Many asked from whence they had come, and how they had learnt their experience in hospital work. On enquiry we found that their order was a modern one, founded by an Irish lady, a Miss Macaulay, in the year 1831. This order in some respects resembles that of the *Sœurs de la Charité*, but differs from it in others; namely, that its members after passing through a two-and-a-half years' noviciate take perpetual vows. The objects of charity to which the Sisters of Mercy

devote themselves arc threefold—the education of the poor, visiting the sick, the
protection of servants out of place; to these are
added others as circumstances require, especially that of the care of hospitals. In
Dublin this work is carried on, and an hospital to be placed under the care of the Sisters
is now in the course of erection. This order,
founded in Dublin, rapidly extended into
many parts of Ireland, and into England and
Scotland; from thence it has spread to Aus-
tralia, New Zealand, America, and California,
and a foundation is now just being about to
be laid in Buenos Ayres.

It was at last decided that Koulali barracks were to be retained for the present as a
British hospital. General Storks therefore
appointed Sister Anne as lady-superin-
tendent.

The general offered us passages in the
"Hydaspes," a vessel belonging to the General Screw Steam Company, and then in the
employ of the government and laden with

shot and shell.   She had for some days been lying off Koulali to coal.

The kindness of all around was very great. The men expressed great sorrow at our leaving and were of course very vexed at the alteration in the hospital routine which was the immediate cause of our departure. When it first took place they thought it must be a great grief to us not to be giving so many " extras," and one day, on going into No. 3 ward, Miss —— found a sheet of paper laid on the table in her ward-room, with some pencilled lines roughly inscribed on it, which were the following—

" Though troubles spring not from the dust
      Nor sorrows from the ground,
    Yet ills on ills, by Heaven's decree,
      In man's estate are found," &c.

This piece of sympathy with a grief, which in reality had no existence, was of course a great amusement to us.   The lady who received it, brought it home at dinner time, and it was of course welcomed with a peal of

laughter. One of the last amusing incidents
that varied our hospital days was the visit of
a French *Sœur de la Charité*. After passing
through the hospital wards, (at the good
arrangement and manifold comforts of which
she expressed great surprise and admiration) we were passing through the main
entrance, and the sentry happened to be a
Highlander. I was passing quietly on when
my companion suddenly stopped and regarded the Highlander with a look of astonishment.

" *Ah ! qui est-ce qui cet homme là ?*"

I answered that he was a Scotch soldier.

" *Ah! que c'est drôle. Je n'ai jamais vu
un costume si bizarre !*"

She then approached the soldier and looked
with great curiosity at his dress. He was
delighted at the sensation he made, and
showed off his accoutrements with pride,
" so sorry " he hadn't his dirk on to show
the lady ; the pouch, however, received such

a share of admiration as ought to have satisfied him.

Dr. Humphrey wrote a letter expressing
his thanks for our services, and there was
not one from whom we did not receive good
wishes.   The "Hydaspes" sailed on the
22nd of November; our preparations for departure were quickly made, and our farewells
said.

We went on board about four in the afternoon, and we could have started immediately,
but the captain was waiting for the Duke of
Newcastle, who did not arrive for some hours
afterwards, and so the moon rose before the
"Hydaspes" heaved anchor.   Between our
ship and the shore lay a large coal barge;
over this one or two of the soldiers chose
to climb, that they might say a last " good-
bye."   A group of them stood on the shore
and cheered us on.

The moonlight lit up every familiar spot,
as we gave a farewell look to dear Koulali,

with which pleasant memories must ever linger. It was some great Turkish *fête*, and the Bosphorus was brightly illuminated as we passed down it.

It would be a needless repetition to describe our *route* as far as Malta. We found a most delightful change in being on board an English vessel instead of the little crowded French steamer in which we came. The "Hydaspes" is a beautiful ship; it was such a pleasure to walk on her broad smooth decks, and our cabins and the saloon were most comfortable. We received much kindness from all, and especially from Captain Baker, who did everything in his power to make the voyage pleasant to us.

The weather was favourable till we reached Malta, with the exception of one night, in which a gale arose and the cargo of shell was in some way loosened and caused the vessel to roll sadly.

November 27th.—We anchored at the

quarantine harbour, Malta, and next day we went into the grand harbour. We remained a week at Malta; the captain's orders being to discharge the cargo of shot and shell there.

The two principal harbours are divided by an oblong peninsula on which is built a castle. Malta is strongly fortified in every direction; these fortifications were built by the knights of St. John, who were masters of it 273 years. The improvements wrought by them were very great, for when Charles V. had offered it to them its barrenness made them hesitate in accepting the gift, while now its means of defence and cultivation are remarkable.

On each side of the harbour is a fortified town; the capital of the island is La Valetta, called after its founder, John of Valetta, a grand master. The town opposite Valetta sustained a severe siege in 1565 from the Turks, but they were completely repulsed, and the town was named Citta Vittoriosa.

Valetta, even after all the sights we had seen,
was quite new to us; the long flights of
steps, the white stradas, tall white houses, and
innumerable churches were a complete contrast to the East.   The great interest, however, attached to Malta, consists in the fact
of its being the " island called Melita," which
received St. Paul after his shipwreck.

The dress of the Maltese women is very
peculiar—it is entirely black; the upper
and middle classes wear black silk, and their
head-dress is called a *faldette*; it is a large
piece of silk made exactly in the shape of
an apron, but one side stiffened with whale-
bone; this is thrown over the head and
shoulders, and held by the hand.   The very
poor women have their dress and *faldette* of
coarse material, but always black, and the
faldette is universal.   Indoors the Maltese
ladies wear colours.   It is said that the black
dress is worn in discharge of a vow made in
time of famine or plague that they should
wear black for two hundred years, and that,

this period being nearly past, they think of changing it; but we hoped it was not true, for it would be a pity indeed that this national and excessively picturesque dress should be laid aside.

Valetta is full of traces of its former governors, the knights. Countless churches built by them, the palace of the Grand Master, the hospital, museum, and public library, all bear witness to their skill and industry; and, when one remembers that they held the island on the condition that they would sustain a perpetual war against the Turks and corsairs, one wonders how they found any time and money to spend at home.

The great monument of their labours in Valetta is the church of St. John the Baptist. This saint was the patron of the order. Their original name was Hospitalliers of St. John of Jerusalem, at which city they were founded in 1100. They served hospitals, but considered their duty also called them to fight against the infidels. They took an active part in the Crusades. It was not till they had wrested the island of Rhodes from the Saracens in 1308 that they assumed the title of Knights. They were then called Knights of Rhodes till they lost that possession in 1522, and, soon after coming to Malta, were named Knights of Malta.

We were disappointed with the exterior of St. John's church, but on our entrance were fully satisfied. What must it have been in the days of old, when all the colouring and gilding on the walls and the frescoes on the roof were fresh, and the choir was filled with the knights in their robes, and their golden cross enamelled in white, with its eight points, in token of the eight beatitudes, and their glittering armour, and when their full chorus rang out gloriously the vesper psalms? Now the beauty has faded, and a few priests and boys chant instead of that mighty peal of praise.

The flooring of St. John's is said to be perfectly unique. It is mosaic, each slab forming a monument to a Knight of St. John. There are 400 of these. At the east end of the church is a large sculpture of the baptism of our Lord. The figure of St. John Baptist is very good. The immense marble pillars are magnificent. The roof is fresco, representing scenes in the life of St. John.

In the side aisles are a number of little chapels; in the south aisle is the chapel of the Blessed Sacrament. This chapel is enclosed by chased silver gates of great beauty; it is hung with red silk, and the lights are so well arranged that a soft roseate glow is thrown upon the silver gates and the altar, having an exceedingly lovely effect. Opposite this chapel, in the north aisle, is the Lady Chapel, which was once enclosed by golden gates, but they were carried away by Napoleon. The chapel is very small, and of no remarkable beauty.

At one side of the Lady Chapel is a
flight of steps, descending which we reach
the chapel containing the tombs of the Grand
Masters.   There is an altar here, but it is
evidently disused.   Here in different niches
are the sculptured forms of some of the
most celebrated Grand Masters of the Order,
brass plates and inscriptions to others covering the floor.   The principal tombs are of
such as distinguished themselves particularly
during their government of this island.   Here
lie all the earthly remains of those " Cham-
pions of the Cross," before whose dauntless
valour the Saracen so often trembled, and
yet who still bore the lowly title of Master
of the Hospital of St. John, and Guardian of
the poor of our Saviour Jesus Christ.

Wonderful is the history of this grand order,
and most remarkable is it that its destruction
should have been brought about by treachery.
What Solyman could not effect by arms,
Bonaparte accomplished with ciphered letters,

and from that hour the order was virtually extinct; for though its members, scattered in various parts, lived on for many years, its spirit was gone. They had proved traitors to their island and their oaths, and thus the order crumbled away.

Leaving this chapel, and proceeding down the north aisle, we entered a number of small chapels, called respectively the English, French, Italian, and German. In the French is a large recumbent figure of a brother of Louis Philippe, a very good piece of sculpture. In the English chapel the altar-piece is St. Michael casting out the dragon. We wondered whether this or the one in the Bridgewater Gallery is the original, for the picture is exactly the same, only that the one in St. John's is not in such good preservation as Lord Ellesmere's property.

In the south aisle, nearly at the end of the church is a very large chapel, which the guide said was the oratory, and probably was some

chapel used by the knights for their private
devotions; now it is disused. The altar of
coloured marble was well worth notice.
Some of the paintings were also good, but
a marble head of St. John the Baptist,
kept under a glass case, was a most beautiful
piece of sculpture.

We visited St. John's daily as long as we
stayed in Malta, and often spent hours, finding out new beauties at every turn. Valetta
possesses a great number of churches, most
of them raised by the knights, others belonging to religious orders, of whom there are a
great many. Numerous as the churches
were, they all seemed well attended. In the
morning when service was going on they
were thronged; in the after part of the day,
as often as the explorer entered any of the
churches, scattered figures here and there in
their picturesque black dress were always to
be seen, apparently rapt in prayer. Sometimes when the church looked quite empty,

and we went groping through the side aisles trying by the failing light to discover the merits of paintings or architecture, behind some large pillar one was sure to stumble upon a Maltese woman, looking so like a statue in black marble one could hardly believe she was not one. We visited the cathedral church of St. Paul's, which is very inferior to St. John's. The church of the Dominicans is a fine one. When we entered it the long line of monks in their white habits were chanting vespers in full choir without music.

We also went to the church of San Publilus, who is said by tradition to have been St. Paul's first convert in the isle. There is nothing remarkable in San Publilus but the fine site on which it stands; before it is a large square paved with stones. We were told that this square presented an extraordinary scene once. There had been a drought in Malta for two years, and the Maltese women, after fasting and praying for a week, walked in procession to San Publilus and knelt in the square. The spectators assured us that the whole square filled with figures in black presented a most singular spectacle. The women chanted the *Miserere*. Before the spectators had time to reach home the rain descended in torrents.

We stayed nearly a week at Malta, and had time to see all the curiosities of the island. We drove one day to Citta Vecchia. This town was the ancient capital of Malta before the Knights of St. John held the island. It is still a bishop's see, and contains a cathedral and several convents. We visited the former, but found nothing worthy of note. At Citta Vecchia stands the church of St. Paul, and also the cave. Tradition says it is the one in which the apostle lodged after his shipwreck, where he kindled the fire, and where the viper fastened on his hand.

A priest conducted us into the cave ; it
was so dark we could not see our way down
the rugged flight of steps, but on arriving at
the foot of them we did not want any other
light than that which is well contrived by a
chink in the wall. This soft, subdued light
falls on the marble figure of St. Paul, one of
the most beautiful sculptures we ever beheld.
He is extending the right hand, evidently to
show it is unhurt, and the expression of the
face is celestial. The spirit of self-sacrifice
which characterised the great apostle is
written in every line. One of our party
remarked, one could almost fancy that the
lips would move and say, "I have imparted
unto you my own self also."

From the cave we went through the catacombs, from whence it is said there is a subterranean passage to Valetta (a distance of
six miles). These catacombs are very extensive and form a perfect labyrinth. As
far as we could understand our guide, who

spoke very imperfect English, we learnt they were built by the Saracens; and that they were erected long after St. Paul's visit to Malta.

Another day we drove to San Antonio, the governor's palace, and greatly enjoyed our walk round the gardens; the orange trees were loaded with fruit, and many lovely flowers were in bloom. It seemed the only place in Malta where green trees could be seen or cool shade found. The absence of green is a great drawback to Malta; for miles the white houses and the blue sea are the only objects, and the eye gets wearied with the continual glare.

At Valetta we visited the public library and museum; some curiosities and books were there placed by the knights. There were a good many students in the library poring over some ponderous tomes. The librarian could speak broken English, and was very civil in showing all his wonders.

He showed us a broken lamp in the shape of a fish, which he said had come out of the catacombs at Rome, and had been used by the early Christians. In the library we were delighted by some illuminated MSS. of great age, but yet in perfect preservation.

Another time we visited some ancient ruins which are supposed to be those of a Phœnicean city; but these remains are so few as to be hardly interesting. Malta was first taken by the Phœniceans, who expelled its original inhabitants the Phocians. Returning from these ruins, through a village about two miles from Valetta, our carriage was stopped for half-an-hour by a procession passing through the principal street carrying a large figure of St. Andrew (it was his fête). As the procession reached the church a number of tiny cannons were fired, which seemed to delight the populace. We had not time to do more than look into the church, which was crowded. Around the altar stood a large number of men in the dresses of the various confraternities, who had carried the figure, and who now held lighted tapers.

The body of the church was one dense mass of women, whose dress being, as before described, entirely black, with the graceful faldette, had a striking effect. Outside the church were many more women and men all kneeling on the ground and seeming rapt in devotion. As soon as the cannon were fired we were allowed to proceed on our way. The shops in Malta are very attractive, especially those hung with the Maltese lace, and others adorned with jewellery; the Maltese crosses in gold or silver filigree work are extremely pretty. Quantities of jewellery are displayed in Valetta, and apparently much prized by the ladies, who do not consider gold watches, chains, bracelets, and rings inconsistent with their sombre garb. We visited the Military Hospital, which is situated near the sea.

The building was erected by the knights, and is a large and commodious one. Some of the wards are of great extent. It seemed well arranged, but the medical officers told us that, though standing apparently in so good a situation, in reality it is one of the worst that can be conceived—being damp and unhealthy. The Malta Hospital is a regimental one, conducted on its routine, and therefore not supposed to contain many serious cases, but the surgeons told us that they had had a great deal of sickness since the war broke out, and one did not wonder at this when we saw the troops of young recruits from England who thronged the stradas of Valetta, who were such *little boys*, that how they managed to be of the right height we could not think—no wonder they soon fell sick in a foreign country. There was a review at Valetta one day in honour, I suppose, of the Duke of Newcastle, who had left the "Hydaspes" on her arrival at

Malta, and, after paying the Governor a short visit, returned to England by the overland route. The review took place in a large square, and was a very pretty sight, though it made us rather melancholy to see all the brave soldiers who were on their way to battle, and perhaps death. Sometimes, though, when walking in the stradas, we could hardly avoid a smile at the pride with which the boy soldiers, both privates and officers, walked about in their new uniforms, and we thought how very dim their beauty would become after a few weeks' roughing it in the East.

December 2nd we sailed from Malta, and on the 10th anchored off Gibraltar. We saw the magnificent fortress under a most favourable aspect, for the last three weeks before our arrival had brought incessant rain, so that Gibraltar was covered with verdure where generally the rock is very arid and bare. We went on shore and climbed up the steep hill to the galleries of the fortifications. These are built in the solid rock. The stone through which they are cut is so humid that in wet weather it drops with water; thus we found ourselves in a perfect shower of *rain*, and so put up our umbrellas, and waded through it. We reached St. George's Hall, which is a large space, with a good many cannons ranged round. All along the gallery are portholes, in which are cannon.

From these fortifications we looked down on the sea, the distant mountains of Africa, the town of Gibraltar, and the neutral ground, which, from the rainy weather, was quite a swamp. On one end of this ground stand the English sentries, on the opposite the Spanish. Descending from the fortifications we passed an old Moorish tower, built when the Moors held possession of Spain.

The rain began to fall in torrents, we were tossed about in the boat which conveyed us

back to the "Hydaspes," and were very well
pleased to hear we were not to leave harbour
that night.   Early next morning we were
once more on our way.   We encountered
very rough weather, the screw could not
work in so rough a sea, so we were under
sail for several days, and were driven out of
our course, never entering the Bay of Biscay
at all.   For several days the weather was so
rough we could not stir from our berths.
An attempt to cross the cabin was quite
dangerous.   We again congratulated ourselves that we were on board so good a ship
as the "Hydaspes;" which bravely withstood
the storm.

One night the gale was so strong that a
sailor was blown overboard, and the sea ran
so high that all attempt to save him was
useless.   At length fine weather returned,
the screw was put in motion, and we neared
the end of our voyage.

On December the 16th we were called on

deck late in the evening to see the Start Light, the first glimpse of Old England. On December the 17th the " Hydaspes" cast anchor off Spithead, and in a few hours more, with very thankful hearts, we were safely at home. One short year only had passed since I left it, but the events of many had been crowded into it.

Here my narrative might end, but that I feel sure my readers will be interested in knowing the fate of those left behind, and especially whether Koulali Hospital continued in its former occupation.

CHAPTER XV.

Koulali Hospital—The Sappers and Miners occupy the Turkish Barracks—Cholera amidst the German Legion in Scutari Barracks—Koulali Barrack Hospital handed over to the German Legion—Arrangements with respect to the nursing staff—Dismantling of the Church Ward—A magnificent storm—A perplexity—Crowded quarters — Accounts from Balaclava—Another Sister gone to her rest—Love and sympathy—Reflections on the nursing in the Eastern hospitals—English hospital nurses—Reasons against the permanent employment of ladies as nurses — Hospital life behind the scenes—The toil of nursing — The spirit in which it should be undertaken.

AFTER our departure the fate of Koulali was decided. Sister Anne found the remaining staff of five ladies and ten nurses more than sufficient for the work of the hospital under its present regulations. All went on very smoothly for about a fortnight, the only difference being that the Turkish barracks were given over to the mounted Sappers and Miners, which added greatly to the bustle of the scene—the once quiet road to the Ladies' Home being now thronged with men, horses, and wagons.

During this period a large portion of the German Legion had been sent to Scutari barracks, where in a few days the cholera broke out, numbers dying daily; the troops were immediately marched out and encamped about three miles from Scutari, where they remained ten days. When the wet weather commenced, it was considered absolutely necessary they should have better protection than a tent, and accordingly on the 4th of December the purveyor-in-chief rode over to Koulali from Scutari with an order from General Storks for the handing over of the Barrack Hospital at Koulali to the German Legion, and the removal of the greater part

of the British sick to Scutari, retaining
only the Convalescent Hospital for the use
of those patients who were unable to be
moved at present, and these also, on their
recovery, were to join the rest at Scutari,
it being intended for the future to keep up
the Convalescent Ward for those patients
only who should be put on shore there,
when it was impossible to land them at
Scutari, which was often a difficult matter to
accomplish during the winter.

Three medical men were to remain in
charge of this hospital, and, the services of
ladies and nurses being of course no longer
needed at Koulali, General Storks intimated
that Miss Nightingale would make arrangements with Sister Anne about engaging those
ladies and nurses who might feel inclined to
accept her (Miss Nightingale's) rules and
wish to join her staff at Scutari in preference
to returning to England. This was accordingly settled in the course of the day.

Sister Anne also sent a messenger immediately to the embassy at Therapia, informing
Lady Stratford of the sudden changes in
the hospital. A violent storm, however,
which came on that evening made it impracticable for Lady Stratford to visit Koulali
before the final closing of the hospital. Dr.
Freeth, the English chaplain, took advantage
of a lull in the storm to visit the embassy
and explain matters to her ladyship, who
sent word by him that she fully intended
coming to Koulali the next day; but the
storm recommencing her intention was frus-
trated. The caidjees were obliged to land
Dr. Freeth at a village a short distance
from Koulali, where the party at the Home
were anxiously looking out for his return,
fearing that from the violence of the storm
he might be in danger.

As it was important the Germans should
come to Koulali immediately, the bustle and
confusion in the hospital were very great.

Everything had to be packed up and removed to Scutari. The dismantling of the linen stores was rather provoking, they had been so neatly arranged and completely filled up with everything that was necessary for the men's comfort and convenience. It was half laughable and half annoying to see the "fatigue party" tumbling down the things to take them to the purveyor's stores.

Sister Anne superintended the packing up of the church furniture and fittings, all of which were free gifts from friends in England. She was one of those who had taken great interest in their arrangement, and it was painful to her and others also to see their once neat little church dismantled in a few minutes.

Then came the packing up of the ladies' free-gift store, and this was no little trouble and labour. One of the officers informed Sister Anne that Captain Macdonald wished to have the key of the ladies' store that same

evening; she replied that was quite impossible, and that it was unreasonable to expect
that everything could be done in a moment.
The officer expressed his regret at being
obliged to hurry her so much, but begged
her to remember that he was "not one of the
kickers, but one of the kicked," as he was
himself obliged to turn out, as well as the
rest of the British officers, to make way for
the German ones, the General's orders on the
subject being urgent. Mr. Robertson coming
up at this moment, and Sister Anne explain-
ing the difficulty to him, he immediately
assured her that the General had no wish
whatever that she or any of the party should
be annoyed or flurried, and that the key must
be waited for till it could be conveniently
given up.

About eight o'clock the storm before
alluded to commenced, and it was described
as one of the most magnificent sights ever
witnessed; the lightning was brilliant beyond

conception; the night had become suddenly dark, but, as flash followed flash, not only the Bosphorus, but objects on the European coast also, were distinctly visible. The light itself was of a peculiar dark crimson colour, at times fringed with purple, and everything at times became as distinct as by the light of day.

Notwithstanding the beauty of the scene, however, it was impossible to help looking with much anxiety on the Bosphorus raging in its most stormy mood, remembering that Miss Nightingale, who had been at Koulali making arrangements with the ladies, was at that moment on its waves in a small caique, as it was impossible she could have reached home ere the storm began, and it certainly is anything but a safe position to be on the Bosphorus in a caique even when the water is far less agitated than it was at that time. They heard next day that the storm met her halfway to Scutari, but that she arrived in perfect safety, though completely drenched, for the rain descended in sheets of water.

The next day the packing continued, as it was hoped in a day or two to leave the Home, which was on their departure to be converted into quarters for the British officers still remaining at Koulali; but the Bosphorus continued to rage so violently that no boat, lighter, or even steamer could come from Scutari, and the goods sent there in a lighter on the Thursday before were two days before they could land their contents. A report reached the Home that one steamer bound for Koulali was wrecked on the way. The road to Scutari was almost equally impracticable. It was difficult for a rider to accomplish the journey, much less a vehicle of any kind.

In the meanwhile what was to become of the British officers, who, by the arrival of the Germans, were now turned out of house and home? Sister Anne at once offered

them some of the apartments at the Home,
reserving as few as possible for her staff of
ladies and nurses.   This offer was gratefully
accepted, and accordingly Dr. Freeth, the
English chaplain, Father O'Dyer, the Catholic
one, Dr. Humphrey, the principal medical
officer, Major Heaton, the commandant, and
two or three of the other medical officers,
took up their abode in our once quiet little
Home, and no doubt the scene was amusing
enough.

The whole party dined together, and as
the storm lasted the whole of the next week,
and the work of the Hospital was over, they
were somewhat dependent on each other
for amusement.   Dr. and Mrs. Tice also
joined the party, and all did their best
to contribute to the general comfort, and to
make the best of circumstances which were
unavoidable.   The time passed pleasantly
enough.   One of the party had a bagatelle
board, and thus helped to while away the
idle hours.

At length after ten days' duration the storm ceased, and the sun shone out with really summer-like splendour. The next morning Captain Macdonald sent a steamer to convey the ladies and nurses to Scutari. Sister Anne returned to England in the Cambria, under the kind escort of Lord and Lady Napier. Some of the other ladies and nurses also returned in the course of a week or two, a few remaining with Miss Nightingale at Scutari.

From Balaclava favourable accounts continue to be received. The Sisters bravely withstand the rigour of a Crimean winter; looking on the bright side of everything they go cheerfully on working for God, and trusting all else to Him. But since we have been safe in our English homes, many a thought has travelled to those parts in which, amidst cold and rain, far severer than any we experience in England, the Sisters dwell.

The rumours of peace were joyful news

to us, bringing with them hopes that ere long, their work done, the Sisters also may return to their peaceful convent homes; but while we were rejoicing over these thoughts the news reached us that one more had already finished all earthly labour, and had gained the shore of everlasting rest. She was the one mentioned in these pages who watched by poor Fisher's dying bed, and who won the especial love of all by the peculiarly holy calm that was ever round her. She was advanced in years, and had devoted her whole life to the service of God in deeds of charity.

She caught fever in her ward and was ill for one week. Great hopes were entertained of her recovery; but at last she sank under her malady. One night in February the Sisters watched around the dying bed, a violent storm arose, which threatened to unroof the hut with every blast that swept over it, but she heard it not. Mingling with the tempest's roar went up the prayers for the dying, and as they bade the " Christian soul depart in peace," she passed away, gentle in life— peaceful in death. The day following was Sunday; and in the evening they bore away the mortal remains of Sister Mary Elizabeth to lay them by the side of Sister Winefrede.

Before the funeral commenced, some of the *Sœurs de la Charité* from the Sardinian camp came with love and sympathy to their Sisters in Christ. Neither band knew the other's language, but united in the language of one common faith, they joined together in prayer. Soldiers of the 89th regiment carried the coffin, followed by the Sisters, a Sister of Mercy and a Sister of Charity side by side. They passed through the double file of soldiers, all with heads uncovered. The coffin rested in the chapel, where seven priests chanted the burial service.

The chapel was crowded two hours before the service commenced. When the coffin was carried forth the concourse was immense.   Medical officers and the Lady Superintendent of St. George's Hospital attended.   It must have been pleasing to the Sisters under their affliction to witness the love and respect paid to the memory of their lost sister by all.

A strange resting-place on the brow of that rugged hill is it for those two gentle Sisters.   Around them lie the bodies of many who have fallen in deadly combat, and *they* too have fought a good fight, and have not been afraid to lay down their lives in Christ's service.   They sought not the praise of men, and now they have found their reward—

> " For they beneath their Leader,
>   Who conquered in the fight,
>   For ever and for ever
>   Are clad in robes of white."

And now we will leave the Sisters of Mercy at Balaclava, trusting that God will keep them, and in His good time bring them home in safety.

The rejoicings for the blessings of peace
will, we trust, ere long resound throughout
the length and breadth of Europe, and thus
will of necessity terminate the nursing in
our Eastern hospitals.   With an emergency
it was suddenly organized, and will thus naturally find its end—but its effects will not
so soon, we trust, pass away.

Attention has been drawn towards the class
of women whose task it is to nurse the sick of
England.   These pages will in some degree
show how unfitted they are for that respon-
sible office.   For though a military hospital
was the worst imaginable position in which
to place them, yet those who were unable to
resist its temptations are certainly unfitted
for their present occupation.

Regarding the ladies who went out various
opinions have been entertained.   Perhaps in
this case their own view of their position
may be the best, as they learnt their knowledge by experience, and most of them agreed

that though in the great emergency that had called them forth their efforts had been blessed to the relief of much suffering, the system was based on no permanent footing. To raise the occupation of a nurse to a higher standard, to form a body who will both nurse in our home hospitals as well as be ready to attend the sick in the army and navy, other means are required.

There are two reasons which may be alleged against the permanent employment of ladies. For the arduous duties of an hospital (especially in a foreign country) long training is required ere the health can endure them. The neglect of this precaution will cause a waste of many valuable lives, while the amount of good for which they will be sacrificed will be but small. Again, experience is necessary for the attainment of skill in nursing, and it is therefore necessary nurses should be changed as seldom as possible. But this is simply unavoidable

when they are ladies possessing home ties
and duties which they are only enabled tem-
porarily to relinquish.   Of course there are
exceptions to this as well as all other objec-
tions which may be raised against the plan,
but I speak not of small or isolated efforts, I
speak of a supply to the present great deficiency of nurses for the poor of England.

How small has been the number of women
sent to the military hospitals of Scutari,
Koulali, and Balaclava.   142 in all,* and of
these only 55 were volunteers—27 ladies,
28 Sisters of Mercy,† and of these only 17
ladies and 20 Sisters were on the spot at one
time, while in the French and Sardinian services there have been hundreds of *Sœurs de
la Charité.*

But, I repeat, it is not for military hos-

---

* I do not speak of either Smyrna or Renkioi, with
the numbers of whose nursing staff I am unacquainted.

† There were thirty-three ladies in all, but six of
these received payment.

pitals alone that we want better nurses.
War, it is hoped, has almost passed, and its
trials and troubles too; but as long as this
world continues, suffering will go on, and
will prevail to its greatest extent among the
poor ; and shall England, who proudly
boasts her superiority in science, government, and wealth above other nations, be
behindhand in alleviating the bitter sufferings of her own children ?

Many who will read these pages have
perhaps never passed within hospital walls,
many more, if they have done so, have paid
their visit at appointed times when all looked
its best. But others as well as myself have
learnt our experience of hospital work from
more authentic sources. We have *lived* in
hospital wards, going there for the purpose
of preparing ourselves—first, to undertake
the nursing of the poor at home, and again
when about to proceed to the East.

We placed ourselves under the hospital

nurses, receiving our instruction from them,
and, thus being possessed of no authority
over them, were admitted behind the scenes
of hospital life; and what we saw there—of
disobedience to medical orders and cruelty
to patients—would fill pages, and make
those who read them shudder! shudder as
we often have done when we saw some little
innocent child, who from some terrible accident had been brought into the hospital, exposed to that atmosphere of evil. More evil
was heard in one hour in a London hospital
than would meet one's ears during months
passed in a military one.

One word must be said for the nurses.
Their work is no light one. The founder
of the Sisters of Charity deemed that the
attendance on all the loathsome diseases
of mankind should exempt his daughters
from practising any of those austerities
which are enforced on religious commu-
nities. It is no easy task to bear with

patience the endless fretfulness of hundreds
of sick, to listen to long complaints with
real sympathy, and speak soothing words
when body and mind are alike worn. To
stand by the sufferer when about to undergo
some fearful operation, to maintain a cheerful spirit when the familiar sounds are those
of moans, of sufferings, or sharp cries of
agony, while the very atmosphere is impreg-
nated with disease. To be firm in carrying
out the doctor's commands when they are a
torture to the patients, and yet gentle and
self-sacrificing in all that concerns themselves. While watchful care must be taken
that familiarity with the sight and sound of
suffering does not bring that hardening to it
which is apt to creep over even a naturally
tender nature, and which is one great cause
of the cruelty and neglect practised by
hospital nurses. No, a good nurse must
receive every new case of affliction as though
it were her first. Yet all this and far more

would be the portion of a hospital nurse. Can any believe that the love of gain or mere kindliness of heart can accomplish this ? Generous impulses, enthusiasm, and benevolence, were called forth by stirring accounts of the suffering of our country's heroes, and bore many forth to struggle through a time which, like that of all passing distress, was one of great excitement ; but the spirit that can go through long years of preparation—that can relinquish the fair things of this world to attend upon the grievously afflicted—must be the one of love springing from the sole desire to follow His steps, who came "not to be ministered unto, but to minister."

THE END.

Printed in Great Britain
by Amazon.co.uk, Ltd.,
Marston Gate.